The Physical Game

A Pickup Coach's Complete Guide To Approach,
Physically Lead And Bed Women

Osvaldo Peña Garcia

AuthorHouse™ UK Ltd.
500 Avebury Boulevard
Central Milton Keynes, MK9 2BE
www.authorhouse.co.uk
Phone: 08001974150

© 2010 Osvaldo Peña Garcia. All rights reserved.

No part of this book may be reproduced, stored in a retrieval system, or transmitted by any means without the written permission of the author.

First published by AuthorHouse   7/27/2010

ISBN: 978-1-4520-0664-2 (sc)

This book is printed on acid-free paper.

Contents

Part One: An Introduction

   1. Why You Must Get Physical Now And Not Wait   11

Part Two: First Things First – How To Start An Interaction From Zero

   2. On Attraction And Starting Conversations (Part 1)   25
   3. On Attraction And Starting Conversations (Part 2)   41

Part Three Getting Physical

   4. The Benefits Of Physical Game   61
   5. Why We Don't Get Physical   71
   6. The How-To's   79
   7. The Infamous Ways Of Getting Physical Fast   99

Part Four: The Internals For Physical Game

   8. Belief System Transformation   111
   9. Perception Is Reality   125
   10. How To Become Fearless   138

Part Five: Closing The Deal And Trouble Shooting

   11. High Energy Game   159
   12. Loud Music, Bitches And Rejection: Frustration In The Game   174
   13. Closing The Deal And Extractions   189
   14. The Pitfalls   206

Part One: An Introduction

The Disconnected Player: An Introduction

Mark is in his mid-twenties and he has had one long-term relationship, which crashed and burned after a year and half. He finishes work and goes home and wonders when he is going to start dating again. How in the world is he going to meet a girl? With a time consuming job and no friends, he gets frustrated. His last relationship lasted four years and left him disappointed and lonely. He had a bad break up and he didn't even like her to begin with. He sees girls he likes on the tube, on the street, at clubs when he goes on company dinners – but he doesn't have the courage to walk up to them. He doesn't even know how to start.

John is in his mid-thirties and has had enough of girls. He has grown both frustrated and disappointed with his love life. He has had four long-term relationships in his life and he married the last girl out of desperation. He thought he had to get married because it was time. Of course, like most decisions made out of desperation, his marriage was a bad one and ended in divorce. John has found himself back at square one. Not only does he have no friends (his friends were her friends), but he has found himself unable to meet new people – let alone girls he likes. He sees girls he likes on the tube, on the street, at the clubs and when he goes on company dinners but he doesn't have the courage to walk up to them. He doesn't even know how to start.

Kevin, 18, a virgin (fondling a girl doesn't count) has just started college. Shying away from social interaction, he reads a lot. He thinks he is not cool enough to hang with the popular kids at the college parties. He sees cool guys getting laid with all the hotties and he wonders how they do it. He wants to know. He goes on the web and discovers "How To Pick Up Girls" discussion forums. He reads for months and learns all the theory there is to know, but still cannot approach a single girl. He is a gun loaded with techniques, tactics and Pick Up jargon – but cannot fire a single shot. He sees girls he likes on the tube, on the street and at the college bar, but he doesn't have the courage to walk up to them. He doesn't even know how to start.

Steve is 22 and very shy. Never had a serious date in his life. He blames it on his looks and the fact he doesn't have any social skills. He spends half the day surfing the internet and the other half studying or playing computer games. He has almost zero friends. Girls don't notice him because he shrinks from public places. When he talks to a girl he cannot find the right thing to say and ends up talking about logical stuff that makes her yawn. He would like to meet a girl and have sex with her – he is horny. He masturbates to porn. He sees girls he likes on the tube, on the street and at the college bar, but he doesn't have the courage to walk up to them. He doesn't even know how to start.

Those guys above are my demographics in a nutshell. I help men who struggle. Some of them have spent so much time at the bottom of the dating barrel that they don't want to leave it. Misery gets to be comfy. Mostly, I have to yank them out of it. Some of them have come to think they cannot get girls no matter what they do. They think it's a curse. Since 2005, I have dedicated my life to changing their minds. I teach guys how to get girls.

At first I liked it, then hated it, and later on I came full circle and started enjoying it. I started believing in my work. Like my girlfriend says: "You are making the world a better place. You are bringing happiness to those people."

Corny? You bet.

But I had not looked at it this way until she pointed that out. I saw myself more like a mechanic fixing a broken car. I never stopped to see the cars racing at 200-miles-an-hour as a result of my work.

Weekend in weekend out I teach live "in-field" programs that transfer the ability to approach and attract women. My work starts on Friday at 7pm and it is not over until Sunday evening. Fieldwork is done in clubs, bars, streets, shopping malls, etc. After my programs, guys not only change in terms of getting more girls, but also transform their lives in the process. Changes in this area have a domino effect into others like business, financial, mental health, physical health and family relations.

I don't have all the answers. I have never claimed I had them. I am not a self-proclaimed guru, nor do I endorse such behaviour. I am simply a coach. I plan to teach you the gist of my experience – the very things I teach on my program. I decided this knowledge could help people if I put it in simple words and avoided all the jargon I have seen on the internet and various Pick Up "subcultures".

I thought I could create a guide for the layman because I think anybody can learn these things if they are simply put. Over the years, and after teaching hundreds of guys around the world, I have developed tools and concepts, which will facilitate the process of Pick Up for regular guys. This book contains the best advice I can give.

You Are A Chump With Women... So What Else Is New?

I am not going to tell you the story of how I went from chump to champ – how I sucked at the beginning and how today I bed women three ways with ease. I just think that kind of story has been rehashed so much it is not worth the effort. But I can tell you it can be done and it doesn't take much. In fact, I do it every weekend: I turn guys into approaching-machines capable of doing anything and everything.

Rather than indulging in a bunch of "kiss and tell" stories, I will tell you how you can use the different techniques and tactics I coach on my programs. Tactics that have already made many others successful.

Starting From Scratch: The Personal Transformation

I don't want to give you the impression this is only for a few guys with special talents or skills. A guy like me – or anybody with success in this game – goes out and repeats certain things, which at the end of the day or night make him successful. Unlike amateurs, successful pros have a certain routine, a certain way of doing things they recycle and pay attention to.

Same when you learn Pick Up. You are going to have to learn a number of things and redo them every night. Just like on a fishing expedition, you go out every night, throw the line and the hook overboard and come home with some fish. In the reiteration of your fishing routine you become a fisherman. Just like fishermen, you must duplicate what you learn here and you will bring home fish.

Most guys ask themselves how hard they must work before they can Pick Up girls for real. Inexperienced as they come, the average guy enrols in my program having never approached a single girl before. They have no idea what they are getting into. As it turns out, they all go through a process of positive transformations on a single weekend that take them from being insecure dudes to cool, confident males around the opposite sex.

Today a whole new dawn of techniques, sophisticated drills and self-actualization exercises will not only speed up your learning process, but also get you laid while practicing. No more long string of rejections before you get laid. No more tiresome practice of routines and openers. Training wheels are off from day one with these new techniques and drills for teaching Pick Up. We have stripped down unnecessary things, streamlined our teaching techniques, and dropped all unnecessary garbage to get you from A to B faster.

Taking Action! The Simple Truth

Contrary to popular opinion you don't have to learn 1000 different things. Action is your word. Doing something, approaching a girl by saying something dumb even, will get you started on this transformation.

Pick Up can be defined as the simple act of walking up to a girl and starting a conversation. At times it doesn't require more than five minutes before she starts showing interest. In fact, girls show interest in most guys after they start approaching hardcore.

Plenty of times, a guy just walks up to a group of people and they have a girl interested in no time. To get women (unlike defusing a nuclear bomb), you just need to employ the right actions; not vast amounts of sophisticated manoeuvring.

Then again, our logical brain kicks in and starts telling us: "Wake up, too good to be true"; that you have never been good with women and you can't do it.

But if you study hard enough, read enough books and internet materials, and watch Pick Up DVDs for advice, you might be able to get it right some day.

If you are thinking in that negative way, you are a victim of the rampant complication syndrome, which afflicts most guys in this game. Most people think that in order to get good, they must learn lots of

Pick up lines, prepare funny and interesting things to say, and memorize loads of tactics. However, the results speak for themselves – guys with the most information finish last.

From Disconnection to Being Emotionally In Tune with Females

I will take you on a journey from not being able to talk to a female to being able to just walk up and start a conversation by talking about anything. By digging into your essential self, we can find topics that we will then use as conversation starters. I will teach you not to try to impress a girl when you first meet, but rather, to express who you are to her.

In the second phase of the book, I will teach you how to get physical – fast. Even within a minute of meeting a girl. I will aid my explanations with real life examples and pictures. Not only that, I will also recommend step-by-step drills I have designed over the years. By getting physical, your interactions will be sexually charged as opposed to dull and just talkative. After a while, thanks to all this interaction with the opposite sex, you will feel a sense of general confidence grow on you. You won't be a stranger to the opposite sex: you will become an attractive man. Other topics will be covered also that are vital to your success with women.

Your Agenda vs. Other People's Agenda

If you don't have a set of default responses when you talk to women in specific scenarios, you will fall victim to those very scenarios. You will be under the thumb of circumstances and circumstances will dictate how you feel and how you respond or live your life.

Many guys have no default reaction to a girl's blowing them off or being rude to them. They become reactive and a victim of circumstances. But you have a choice. In reality you can create your very own default behaviour to a situation like that— from laughing your ass off, to saying thank you to her for being a great sport. You can create those choices. You can have your agenda and enforce it. You can influence the situation rather than let the situation influence you.

If you have your own agenda — a set of default answers to situations, you can influence circumstances out there. I have often sent a student back into a group of girls who had previously blown him off and, to his surprise, the girls have accepted him back and showered him with unprecedented attention. Rather than being a victim of their agendas, we made a choice and influenced the circumstances by going back to them.

I Can Choose My Response

You can sit down and plan how you are going to respond to everyday situations in a club. You can have an action plan for everything that happens to you, and you will be ready to influence your situation and not let your situation influence you.

Most guys march into a night club to approach women expecting that things will work out. They have no real plan or proactive-ness on their side. A pretty hopeless approach when you face the chaotic scenario of a club.

In this book I plan on making you proactive when you have to talk to girls in various circumstances and places. I want you to be ready and have a whole arsenal of default behaviours for every occasion. As a result of this behavioural toolbox, you will feel confident and safe as you make your approach to a girl.

What Is Physical Domination?

When I throw this word physical domination into my seminars, it tends to cause a bit of a concern. No, I don't plan to beat women up with these techniques. However I do plan to teach you how to lead them physically. Like I have said before, women will not take responsibility for the escalation, so we must take charge.

Like I always say, you want to be nice to women but you want to be firm — an apparent contradiction. I don't want you to go around manhandling women like a wrestler but I do want you to be firm when you lead. It means you must anticipate resistance on their side and be ready to plough through it. You will encounter plenty of obstacles in becoming dominant with women. But experience has taught me when you break their resistance, women become much more attracted to you.

How to Manage Your Energy And So Much More...

This book will deal in depth with preserving your energy when you are in a night club and make it last all night. I will deal with how you can avoid the common energy draining pitfalls of approaching. It's key to becoming a top player at this game.

I also plan to walk you through all the steps from meeting a girl to taking her home that same night. I will devote an entire chapter to what's called "pulling". I will make it easy and break it down for you so you can execute it any time you are out there. Not only that, I will teach you how to have fun as you are doing it.

So let's wrap this up and get on with the chapter of the book that will get you acquainted with Physical Game and what it takes to pull it off...

CHAPTER 1

Why You Must Get Physical Now And Not Wait

*Discover Physical Game (PG)
And How It Can Get Your Game Up To the Next Level*

As a coach, it used to be a challenge to explain Physical Game. No amount of live-in-field demos could help students do what I wanted them to do. So, out of frustration, I resorted to visuals like stop-motion videos and frame-by-frame picture exposés.

Then, I saw a huge jump in results. Equipped with a visual image, clients had a frame of reference to build their practice on. With an ever-increasing number of make outs and same night lays on program, I decided to dig deeper into this modality of the game.

I started to work on the "outside" Physical Game and I challenged my students to produce what I call "the look": meaning, what your actions would look like to a bystander. It must look "on." It must look like you and your girl are a unit, a couple, hooked up, together. I want your girl to think: "Gee, I don't know, but it looks like I am all over him." But in reality you are all over her.

Women can feel a rush when you apply Physical Game and lay it down hard — the way I plan on teaching you in this book. Simpler than you think, PG should be applied within seconds of starting your interaction. A typical comment I get from guys is: "I never thought it was that simple."

As it turns out in practice, women love physical contact as delivered by a masculine guy. They reward this behaviour with lots of attraction and giggling. Contrary to popular opinion, women love to be touched. Not by any man, but by a confident, bold guy not afraid to take risks and go for it.

Why People Believe Sweet Talkers Are Good With Women. Destroy the Myth Now!

Indoctrinated by Casanova and Don Juan's legendary exploits, the general population have come to believe good talkers make good womanizers.

Wrong.

Most guys can talk the talk, but can't get laid.

Being physical goes far beyond the reach of words and tales. It makes a statement about you — who you are as a man. It knocks women out. After teaching men to get good with women for five years, I realized an obvious but painful fact: the guys who talked well, were well educated, and had lots of verbal resources, were the ones with the most problems leading a girl to bed.

Unless I stepped in and ordered them to be physical they would not get a make out. In fact, those guys were the ones with whom I had more problems.

On the other hand, guys who couldn't talk that well but got physical fast and couldn't care less if a girl liked them or not, were getting all the women.

We all know many popular beliefs are not based on truth, but on stereotypical ideas never questioned in depth. Don Juan and Casanova's sweet talking are just one of those cultural archetypes never been put to a test of serious inquiry.

Just turn on your TV and you will see plenty of this popular belief being recreated on soap operas and movies: a guy with good looks and precise line for every occasion (think of James bond) gets the beautiful girl every time.

Stop for a minute and think how TV writers create those soaps by rehashing an age-old stereotypical idea: the sweet talking Casanova gets the girl.

TV programs and movies have no time to test anything; they are under pressure to be an overnight success and get the approval of a TV-jaded audience. Therefore, these easy-to-accept ideas find their way into your TV screen and the mental fabric of the population over and over again. They become legitimate over time due to repetition.

"How can Physical Game be more effective?" you may wonder.

Well, it's easy to explain. After careful observation, weekend-in, weekend-out on my live programs, I know getting physical changes a girl's body chemistry. Certain chemicals kick in when you touch somebody with confident and pleasant determination. If you don't believe this, think of a time when a girl's breast brushed past your chest and you got aroused. Her random touch activated a whole bunch of chemicals in your body, "mating" chemicals if you will. I am no chemistry teacher but I can tell you from observation that when a dominant guy grabs a girl, you see her face light up, she starts giggling and she becomes compliant in record time.

Such amazing, too-good-to-be-true things don't happen, you might argue in disbelief. However, I've seen women opening up like flowers. I don't want to get deep into any chemistry lessons here because I want to stick to what works, and not on lengthy scholarly explanations.

In the empiricism of a live-in-field program lies the proof in the pudding. Guys who fail to get physical don't get laid. Yes, they can maintain long conversations with women — even get a phone number — but they miss the boat at converting all that into sex.

Physical Game proves over and over to be the fast track to sex. Verbal game is your slow, "lucky if you get there" lane.

Your Road to Get There. How to Destroy Those Limiting Beliefs. How To Stop Thinking Like Average Guys

You might ask: "How do I become the dominant and physical guy you talk about? I know I have seen many successful guys with women. But I am not one."

Very true.

But – a big *but* – if you are thinking this way, you are like most guys who think of Pick Up as a complicated operation; only few chosen ones can do it because it requires a special kind of person or two to five years of hardcore training.

Wrong.

Why Does This Happen?
Destroy Your Mental Chaos By Following Simple Rules

Dubious internet marketing on "How to meet women" creeps the net. Lots of contradicting theories and Pick Up systems cloud novices' minds to the point of overload. They get confused.

Walking up to women with such mental chaos makes you exude failure. Most guys don't succeed: not because they are bad at it, but because of their confusion in the field. If you are incongruent and incapable of maintaining a normal conversation, a woman will see you are not sure about what you are doing, and so lose interest and walk away.

Correct your mental chaos by walking into the club with only a couple of ideas in your head. You will cut through the bullshit of tons of Pick Up knowledge gathered over time on the web. We are talking about rolling in a crowded venue with a double barrel of simple ideas as opposed to a barrage of dubious contradicting info.

Keep it simple and you will be rewarded with trust from women, attraction and sex. Complicate it and you are asking for trouble. I am saving you months and years of disappointment in this area of your life.

Plenty of times I've met guys who have been going out for years and never gotten past first base with girls. They believed Pick Up was about gathering information: the more the better. But less unnecessary action proves more efficient than running around like a chicken without a head.

So The Question Remains: Can I Do It? Is It For Me?

Whether you have been approaching women for a year or you are just starting off, this information can help you grow faster.

It will make guys who can already start conversations far more deadly in their interactions with females.

It will set guys who are just starting off on the right track and it will shave years off their learning curve. It will ensure bad habits like stalling conversations, not moving things forward and passivity will not set in and slow you down. In other words Physical Game is for everybody and it is a crucial part of getting laid with consistency. Anybody can perform PG if so inclined. In so doing, you accomplish a crucial part of the getting-laid process.

But if I am going to be straight with you, and get your trust from the get-go, I am going to have to disclose the secret of the dating industry.

PSSSST...Don't tell. I will be out of my job!

Here It Is. The Secret They Don't Want You To Know!

Most people believe they must be masters before they can enjoy any type of results. That they will have to put in years of hard practice in clubs and approach thousands of women.

Completely untrue!

You can get laid today without experience if you dare to apply what I am explaining here. There have been guys laid on my program on the first night with zero experience.

Ok, I let the cat out of the sack. Which brings us to your next most common question about physical game.

Will Women Take It?

Will women allow a guy to walk up to them and start getting physical without retorting with some form of resistance?

Fear of rebuttal can deter many guys when they start walking down the physical path. They dread women's reactions or looking bad in front of others. What if I told you women will take it and like it. Hard to believe?

Based on my years of experience taking guys into clubs on live programs, and my personal experience over five years, I can guarantee nothing ever happens. I mean, your old slap across the face, kick in the groin routine. Empirical evidence, live in the field, shows worst case scenarios don't happen. In fact, women are waiting on you to make a physical move on them. Yes, that's right. They are waiting for a confident dude to step in and take them for a physical ride.

In years of practice of PG, aside from grabbing a guy's hand and putting it off their body, women don't reject a physical guy. Exceptions confirm the rule. Therefore rejection must be an irrational fear embedded in our brain. I have seen students do the craziest physical stuff to women in clubs and I personally have performed jaw-dropping stunts without a single sign of rejection. In all fairness, it seems as if they like it and want seconds.

Why You Are Not Your Story.
How To Stop Letting Your Past Determine Your Present

Most guys come from an unsuccessful background with women – one long string of failures or rejections. Your average male finds himself in a Catch-22 of sorts, where the more he tries, the more he doesn't get laid. It's as if there's a tightening noose around his neck and the more he struggles to get out the harder it chokes. In the end, he gives up and stops trying. He starts to rely on luck and alcohol – If he tries at all.

In reality, most males don't get laid. I think the statistic is that an average man has four to seven sex partners in all his life. Some, none. They die virgins. Amazing isn't it? Scary facts crawl out when we dig deep in this area.

I mean! Four to seven sex partners in a lifetime?! Some of the guys I have taught go through two or three women on a weekend. Some lay them in threesome fashion. Crazy, right?

Well there are guys out there living a kind of rock-star sex life as you read this sentence. Those guys have something in common with you: an unsuccessful past with women – they were as desperate as your average dude.

Nothing can be done to change your past, but you can transcend it. Instead of enslaving yourself to your sad life story, you can go out, take action and become one of those guys that come to my programs. Most people feel drawn to their past – so much so it becomes their comfort zone – their present. Doing something different feels like death. They have grown accustomed to getting nothing in this area of their life. Your past, your story, your repeated failures with females have a strong pull. I know as I say this it sounds incredible – but you can change.

The Physical Game

You think that, as a regular guy, you won't be able to make things different, but you are wrong. The guys I teach are as regular as it gets. Accountants, students, waiters, businessmen, actors, soldiers, handicapped guys, ugly guys, unemployed guys; all kinds from all walks of life have tried this and been successful at it. So, yes, you can have a different story. Decisions you make today will make all the difference.

Your Road To Mastery:
How Long Before You Get These Skills Down?

Most guys ask themselves how hard they must work before they can Pick Up girls for real. Back in the day, we used to tell newcomers that the first 2000 approaches don't count. However, our knowledge was very limited five years ago. Today, with the tools and information we possess, the actual learning time is irrelevant. A newbie will get laid all the way to mastering these skills.

Four years ago, we used to teach a different type of game, full of memorization and performance related skills. We used to train guys to be performers, circus monkeys. Yes, it was the dark ages of Pick Up!

Must I Be Perfect To Get Laid?

Not really. You don't have to be a super performer to get girls. I have learned through years of personal practice and teaching that you don't need to be Mr Pick Up to start a conversation with a girl. Beginners get laid as well as seasoned veterans. If you are a beginner you will lay your way into the mastery of your skills. Most guys don't realize this and are afraid to start the long journey of practice without the assurance of tangible rewards. In the end, it prevents them from taking action.

You must not seek perfection. I teach my students to do it poorly, but get it done. Don't expect a flawless performance and you won't be disappointed. You will have freedom to make mistakes, learn your lessons and your learning curve will speed up. Dare to be imperfect and you will learn this game. It takes a guy without an ego and a willingness to take action. Live by the mantra: "good enough is good enough."

Do You Want To Know The Simple Truth Of The Game?

Here it goes. You ready?

During a night out, there will be some girls who will like you NO MATTER WHAT, and others who won't, NO MATTER WHAT. I don't care if you are a seasoned veteran with thousands of approaches under your belt, or a total newbie trying to get your first lay. On any given night some girls will accept you no matter how bad you screw up; and, on your same night, there will be a number of girls who won't care for you, no matter how good or socially savvy you are. Fact.

Like Oliver Stone's movie "On Any Given Sunday," on any given night you can succeed or fail. There are nights where you encounter resistance from every other group. But on others, everything flows. No way around this. Some of my students float to success on the first night of the program, only to find themselves swimming for their lives on the second night — and vice versa. In truth, you cannot predict your outcome let alone become "perfect" on a game based on talking to strangers.

What happens when guys don't get the desired positive or approving reactions?

I tell you what happens: your average Joe walks away with his tail between his legs never to be heard from, or approach another woman again for the rest of the night. At the first sign of trouble, those guys stop trying — which limits their success to none. Because, as you will learn later, a girl's token or knee-jerk resistance comes as a given. If we are to succeed, you must be trained to stop paying attention to signs of approval or lack of it.

The Elusive Obvious

The more you do it, the better you get at it. Simple enough. No need to go to Pick Up University for four years. Just by taking consistent action you will benefit from successive approximation to your goal. The more women you approach, the better you get at approaching. The more women you try to kiss, the better you get at it.

For example, I tell students I want them to pull a girl on the dance floor within the first 30 minutes of being in the club. Just one. But they

The Physical Game

end up with five or six girls. They wind up kissing one or two. Avoid sophistication like the plague and rely on the simplicity of execution. Try Physical Game with every girl and end up with lots of them back in your apartment. Perfect practice makes perfect.

However, and I must reiterate this idea, I am not after perfection, I am after execution.

Why Clubs Are Intimidating and Why We Shouldn't Fear Them

When I first started visiting them, clubs scared me. As I approached a venue's door and saw the bouncers, I felt an uncomfortable sensation in my stomach. I couldn't think of a nice thing to think about. I was more focused on performing well in those days than on having a good time. Having never been a social type, I had a lot of fear of strangers. Therefore, for me, just like for you today, going to a crowded place was very stressful.

In hindsight, my dreadful attitude towards clubs stemmed from the irrational belief that "strangers are a threat." From early childhood, when your mom tells you not to talk to strangers or "stay out of trouble," she embeds in your subconscious an irrational fear of being social. Most people are taught these things as children and it helps them survive childhood. But those learned behaviours become a problem when you face the club.

With time, practice and good results, I learned to love clubs. They were where I had fun, met new, exciting people and got girls. As I grew in the game my new comfort zone was in a club talking to people every weekend– to the point that everything else in my life became less important. I couldn't stay home on a weekend. I had to be out.

Why Clubs? Could I Meet Girls Anywhere?

Like a playground where little children learn to walk, a club provides unparalleled simplicity for practice. We learn to improvise, grow, become better and get laid. Without a club, we would have a hard time finding a place where we can have an unlimited number of women to practice with. In a night venue, women are packed or stacked, if you will, one upon the other. So we can practice at will with zero delay between approaches.

Very much like target practice or shooting fish in a barrel, a club offers unlimited possibilities to get laid because of the abundance of females. I like to think of a club as a small cell that reflects society as a whole. Groups go there to associate and have fun together, which gives ample opportunity to sharpen our skills at approaching people.

It's not only girls. We meet guys too in those groups. And we learn to deal with them too. You might say: "But why guys? I don't plan to sleep with guys." Well, I hope you do plan on becoming a social guy. In order to do that, you must be able to interact with males and females alike. Unless you learn to be social and interact with everybody, this game is going to become extremely hard for you.

"But I Hate Clubs"

Many guys object to clubs because they don't know or haven't yet experienced the benefits of approaching women in clubs. They complain: "It is too loud, too crowded." Or: "The girls are bitchy." To a certain extent, I agree. But you also must not pass up the opportunities such venues have to offer. They provide you with an obstacle course unparalleled by any other type of venue. The more obstacles you jump the faster you learn, and the tougher you become.

Personally, not only do I like to take my students to nightclubs, but I also want to take them to the toughest places with the loudest music and the bitchiest girls. My rationale: after that experience, any other venue looks like a walk in the park. If they are able to survive four hours of non-stop approaching action there, they don't have to worry anymore about smaller and kinder venues like bars, lounges, malls, or coffee shops.

I believe in jumping ever-bigger hurdles as a way to improve yourself faster in the game. It goes back to my experience as a semi-pro baseball player. The tougher the league we played, the better we got as players. We realized that as we moved up our level of play improved too, because we had to adjust our game. Though losing many games in the beginning we ended up adapting to our new league in the end and won many baseball games against tougher opponents. We learned to be patient, not panic, and work every opposing team's weaknesses.

Same for this game. The tougher your playground, the stronger you get inside; and the faster you climb up your learning curve. In my programs, you will feel like you are being thrown in at the deep end of the pool. The more I throw you in there, the faster you learn to swim.

"But I Prefer Daytime Interactions. It Is Easier"

Well, you might have a point there.

Though people tend to be more polite during the daytime, other unforeseen circumstances will hinder your practice. For one, brevity of exchanges will kill you.

Most people are going somewhere during the day. Let's say you meet a girl in the tube waiting for her train. You might be able to strike up a conversation, but you may lose your girl as soon as her train comes unless you are going her direction. In all likelihood, you will end up with a phone number, and a hope she will answer you back – a lot to hope for. Most daytime practitioners report they need an awful lot of phone numbers to get a date with a single girl.

Why?

If we analyse the above tube example, we realize that you don't have enough time to build any kind of trust and rapport with the girl. Therefore, since you are just a stranger who had a five-minute shallow exchange with her, she doesn't feel the urge to return your calls.

In addition, the walking between approaches can compromise your practice. During the day, you spend an awful lot of time walking around finding girls. That means you can start a conversation, and then walk five to ten minutes before your next encounter.

In a night club, where lots of girls are under the same roof, you only have to go from one to the next.

In a packed venue you can do 30 approaches in 90 minutes if you are so inclined. With efficiency guaranteed, the more you practice, the more you learn in less time. It comes as no surprise the top players in this activity learned it first in clubs.

Moreover, at a club you can meet a girl and spend two to four hours together. During the day, you will find yourself unable to go deeper with her in your interaction. Due to the brevity of interactions, you wind up with shallow exchanges. In a club, you have plenty of time to know each other and gain some deep trust and rapport.

Sure, you might take her for coffee after a brief exchange in a shop during the day. However, with scattered exceptions, you will often find after a short interaction, they go about their business. You are at the mercy of luck when it comes to the bogus phone numbers they leave you with.

"Then, Should I Rule Out The Daytime From Practice?"

No. Quite the contrary. You should be able to approach women anywhere and everywhere. You might find girls you like at your grocery store, bookstore, etc. Approach them – but it should be regarded only as your bonus round from the club. Clubs should be your meat and daytime your potatoes. Not very efficient if you turn it around. Clubs can offer you the ultimate place to practice.

But I am getting ahead of myself. Let's start at the beginning. I will teach next how to initiate a conversation first.

Part Two: First Things First –
How To Start An Interaction From Zero

CHAPTER 2

On Attraction And Starting Conversations (Part I)

Why A Closer Starts At The End. What To Say At The Start. How To Get Others Excited About Who You Are. And More...

Why Your Mind Goes Blank When You See A Hot Girl

"Blanking out" ranks at the top of a novice's list of most common problems when approaching a female. Like most "issues" for rookies, it tends to disappear in a hurry after a night of live program. You don't hear it ever again. This nasty "sticking point" vanishes. Let's see how we can solve it in the next two chapters.

I will start with the obvious: social conditioning and your need to impress. As soon as a regular guy sees a hot girl he starts thinking along the lines of: "I must pick her up now." Or: "I must say something funny/witty/smart to get her." Or: "I must do something to get her attention and make her take me seriously." Thinking along those lines will make you fall in your most common trap of Pick Up, the "I must impress" trap. As painful as they come, this knee jerk reaction will thwart your conversational efforts with a woman. You will find girls see through the "I am trying to impress you" persona like a looking glass. Since they have seen it all before the more you try to astound them, the faster they lose interest in you.

Furthermore, in trying to dazzle a girl, you subliminally communicate that you don't deserve her. You are neither entitled to her nor good enough. That's why some jerk types have amazing success with women-because by being dismissive they broadcast their willingness to walk away at any point. Women have no power over them. But unless you have a natural jerk persona to you, I wouldn't recommend you try this approach. Believe me, many have tried to impersonate the jerk with little or no success. Don't walk down that road. No need to.

But let's get back to "trying to impress." When you try to impress, your mind starts to screen what you say. Soon enough, you run out of flabbergasting things to say to a girl. This process may happen in seconds or just three minutes after you start talking to her-time goes fast when you talk to a girl. Now, the hotter your girl, the harder your mind will "screen" for awe-inspiring things to say, the faster you will run out of options.

You, being a regular guy, not Tom Cruise, will bend over backwards to seek for an exciting story – which you don't have. If you keep it up you will find yourself exaggerating parts of your life – otherwise called lying. A Catch-22 of sorts will ensue: you will sink deeper into inauthentic behaviour, causing women to further be repelled by you. You cause a conversation to spiral down when you have nothing solid to talk about.

On top of that, if you see you don't get any positive regard (read approval) out of her, you will get anxious. You will start "Fishing for reactions," as we call it, which tends to make things even worse – and push your girl further away from you. In a desperate attempt to fake confidence, some start talking nonsense or turn dismissive on a girl. Your inadequacy in this situation will be revealed in a painful way.

It all happens because you are trying to tell her all these impressive/funny things about you, and so you subliminally communicate that you don't deserve her for WHO YOU ARE. You also make it obvious that you care about her approval of you- thus, you are alerting her to the fact that she could manipulate you by withdrawing or giving her blessing to you. She has all the power because you give it away. As you dig your hole deeper through further attention seeking, you create a self-fulfilling prophecy of rejection, which descends upon you.

This process reflects your average guy. Let's see what it's like for your average girl.

The more you try searching your head for "dazzling things to say", the more she loses interest in you. Being eye candy, she has seen plenty of "try hard" guys before. In her mind, you join the long string of losers that tried to get into her pants by paying compliments, flashing a Rolex/ a killer job/a great car or adventurous trips to the moon. Business as usual for a hot girl. Others have dealt with this problem before. So let's look at some of the ways we have come up with over the years to overcome it.

Faulty Yet Attractive Solution: Scripted Game

Let's go down memory lane and examine Scripted Game.

As a result of the "mind goes blank" effect, some years ago there appeared Scripted Game. I was one of those guys who fell for it at the time – to a great extent because we had no other working model back then. When you used rehearsed Scripted Game you memorize lines that gave you the confidence you lacked when talking to a girl. Like an actor, you juggled your memory into memorizing long scripts of things to say on the approach. The confidence came from how well you could deliver the lines.

Needless to say, when you forgot the script, or it didn't fit the situation, you found yourself with just enough rope to hang yourself.

All these things were invented back in the day to substitute real confidence. It was kind of a quick fix: the more you recited your lines, the better you got at them, and the easier it was to throw them into any situation. Most guys would not be able to function without the memorized lines. But once the girl gave them some hardcore test that was not in the "script" you were out on a limb to find something to say. You got sent back to square one, the "my mind goes blank" syndrome all over again!

And therein lies the basic flaw of Scripted Game.

How can you fit every human interaction into a tight costume of scripted lines? How can you have a line for every situation that arises in a chaotic environment like a club? Can you develop real confidence under a barrage of Pick Up lines and tactics? How can you grow self reliant in social situations if you use a smoke screen of material to relate to others? The reality was that most guys never became genuinely confident. After years of practice they remained as insecure as they were when they first started. Bummer.

One of the nastiest effects of Scripted Game was what we used to call the "social robot" effect. Guys' personalities could not find their way through the enmeshment of tactics and lines coming from another person – an internet Pick Up guy or guru of sorts. So they ended up substituting their real personalities with a veneer of Game – a facade, a front that was not only unhealthy, but also counterproductive when they tried to talk to real people. Because people notice something "fake" about you. They cannot pin point what, but they can smell something rotten in the state of Denmark.

Not to mention the frustration and boredom a guy feels by parroting the same lines and openers months and years on end. You hear them talk of depression, lack of enthusiasm, misogynistic tendencies or what have you. Saddled with someone else's lines and routines, which have nothing to do with them or their true personality, they end up in mindless repetition night after night. Thus, the "social robot" effect: namely you become a repetition machine with buttons to push and outcomes to get.

I must call your attention to the fact Scripted Game was a reaction to the "my mind goes blank" issue most guys faced when talking to women. It was never intended as a well thought out plan to better express yourself. It was designed to impress, *to get a girl to like you.*

In other words, it was spawned in an attempt to seek approval from a woman. However, the fact remains, when a female detects you want her acceptance, you lose all the power. She can see it all as a ploy to get into her pants. As her interest drops, you join the long line of losers who tried to wow her over the years. You become part of the trash.

Simplicity Rules

I say "simplicity rules" well knowing that most guys will not buy into it. Most guys imagine that getting good with women is a complicated process requiring never ending practice. However, the field proves them wrong on many levels.

You can boil this game down to the bare essentials: "see a girl, approach a girl." Simple as that. And you've got a 50-50 chance she will be all over you in no time. By the way, I hope I don't give the impression approaching is easy. Most guys balk at walking up to a desirable girl. Not easy – but simple. I cannot stress enough that for most guys, if they summon the courage to take the first step and approach a girl, the rest takes care of itself.

But I still haven't told you what you want to hear. Knowing guys as I do, I know what you are thinking right now: "But when is he going to tell me what to say to a girl?" I will let the cat out of the sack in a minute, but I must warn you once I explain Physical Game in detail later on, what you say to a girl becomes irrelevant.

You ready?

Talking is the easy part.

The Solution To The "What to Talk About" Issue – In Five Minutes

Passion, intensity and enthusiasm. The 1-2-3 of approaching girls.

I would like to start with my favourite: passion stories. Find out what you feel passionate about. Think of a real life anecdote around your passion (such as surfing, stamp collection, rock climbing, a favourite hobby) and strip it of negativity and sexual references – just to be safe.

Reality Check

Try to be uplifting when you tell your anecdote. You don't want to bring people down on a Friday night. You can start a conversation and throw your story right after "Hello, my name is..." followed by "Guys, check this (insert anecdote or passion)..." That's it. You won't need much else. You can approach groups for one night like that.

In less than five minutes at my program, I ask all my students to talk about something they feel passionate about. The answers come back with your usual "music, films, etc."

I then dig down deeper and get a personal passion from each person. Something they do in their spare time because they enjoy it. I then ask them to think of an anecdote around their hobby and give them the chance to tell the story to the rest of the students. Other times I give them 90 seconds to sell me their hobby. In this limited time frame, they must convince me – and get me excited about their free time activity. If they don't, I tell them to dig deeper and find a different hobby closer to their heart.

When they hit on a good anecdote closer to home, they start getting animated and expressive. Then I say, "stop" in the middle of their story. And then I turn to the other students and ask: "What's happening now?" To which they reply: "He is talking with passion." And then I ask: "You see the difference?" They say they were getting excited about his passion because he looked excited, and they wanted to know more about the topic of conversation. They were sold on it.

I then do it again with the second thing they feel passionate about so they each have two stories to use for the rest of the night.

Once they have done this, I never hear "what do I say to her?" ever again for the rest of the weekend. When they run out of things to say, they fall back on these passion stories.

By far the simplest of ways to communicate your heart: talk of something that turns you on. I have perfected my "digging" technique so much by doing it every weekend, I can perform this uncomplicated surgery in less than five minutes.

Sometimes, I just say to the guy: "Just go and sell them on windsurfing"(provided the guy loves surfing). The mission: get girls excited about your passion. It doesn't take long to do this if you use your inner, most-cherished, life passions no matter how outrageous. I once had a guy, a kung fu expert, teach girls Tiger Crane kung fu. It was funny to see him on video – I take sneak videos of my students in clubs for feedback purposes the next day – teaching basic kung fu positions to girls in a club. We had a good laugh.

The sky is the limit. You can talk to girls about tap water for all I care as long as it excites you. On a different level, you don't just get girls excited about your story, you get pumped about yourself. When you make her see life through your kaleidoscope, how you see the world, your unique perspective, she gets to meet the real you.

Tell Them Who You Are

You can dig as deep as you want and look for your secret passions and things that refuse to come up on your first scrutiny. If you want to know what gets you going in life, take a moment and analyse your day. Then ask yourself what activity you spend most of your time on, outside your job. What activity makes you forget about time? I call this your "time elastic" activity. Something that makes you forget the ticking clock. When you get that, you found your passion.

For example, you spend all your free time in your gym and shopping for quality food to cook. Then you get it. You might want to talk about healthy cooking and your favourite recipes to girls.

Girls want to see a real person behind the story, his passions and his enthusiasm, his true personality. You must come alive for them.

As a bonus, you don't have to fake congruency or rehearse this because you can talk about your life in your sleep. Since you know it by heart already, there is no need for repetition or practice. You become congruent without trying.

You need congruency in gaining immediate trust and generating interest. You will have them in the palm of your hand the moment you open your mouth. Get excited about yourself and what you have going for you. Average guys take their lives for granted. They overlook the obvious. I have had guys on program with the most amazing lifestyles, but they have been too shy to talk about them to girls for the fear of bragging. Being genuine will prevent you from bragging.

Be A Source Of Good Energy

You cannot punish a girl into liking you. Forget it. Telling her of the impending doom of mankind will do little or nothing to encourage her to jump in bed with you. (Except for the weird ones!) She will get negative and you don't want that. Nobody wants to hear end-of-the-world talk for a simple reason: they have enough of that from the media, their jobs and their shitty lifestyle. In reality they go out to forget how crappy their job/life/the world is. By being a black hole of sorrow, you seal your fate. You will be rejected.

Conversely, you don't want to be the archetype of the nice or goofy guy. Neither gets taken seriously for they become too invested in approval. Once girls get the vibe you seek acceptance with ulterior motives of getting into their pants, they will spit you out of your group faster than a fat kid grabs a donut. You want to be the solid guy, not approval seeking, not afraid to be himself around others and looking for nothing but a good time. People respect and relate to that.

How To Break Your Mental Block: Turn Censors Off

"My mind goes blank" syndrome happens when "censors" get activated because of social pressure. When in front of people, you "watch what you say" – censorship. Designed to get you approval in gregarious situations and stop you from screwing up, censors work as a traffic light for survival in society. A red light stops the traffic of words when external sources threaten to disapprove of your conversation. You won't go far in society unless you get some kind of approval. That's how your mind works in the office, at school, at home.

Well, that's how your mind works inside a club too, out of habit. In turning those "acceptance seeking" censors off lies the solution to allow you to blast through pervasive social conditioning. Say whatever you feel like saying. Don't question it. Be assertive. Say what you mean and mean what you say. People will respect you more for it. You will respect yourself more for it.

By turning those nasty "people pleasing" filters off, you arrive at a new freedom. A freedom to express yourself without holding back must rule your actions instead. Say whatever you feel like saying without caring about consequences. Give your honest opinion on things without dreading that a disapproving boss will fire you. In fact, nobody will know about it the next day.

Reality Check

People in clubs are strangers. Those survival mechanisms from the real world become irrelevant in a club. You don't have to survive in there. Strangers have no hold over you. It doesn't mean you must go around insulting people, but it means you can let your voice be heard. You are free.

"I Need An Opener"

Do you?

Opening lines were invented because guys needed an excuse to approach a woman. "I need a reason to approach a girl," summarizes in a nutshell how inexperienced guys think when they face a club.

Quick answer: you don't.

Most guys are under the impression that girls will find out their ulterior motives, so they need to hide their true intentions with "a reason to talk to them." However, in any social gathering, even in a regular day-to-day scenario like a supermarket or a crowded bus, you don't need a reason to approach a girl.

Just one of the skills you need: walking up to people without a "why." and chatting them up like you would at a friend's party. Do you have an opener/reason to talk to people when you throw a party in your own backyard? Imagine yourself in your own backyard. Think of the club as the interior of your own house. Would you still need a reason to start a conversation? You wouldn't mind walking up to anybody in your own house, would you?

After attaining normalcy, becoming social and steering clear of "weird" Pick Up stuff, you will see that people form a different attitude towards you and get deeper into conversations with ease. Instead of sweating over interactions, you will find people eager to hang around you. For starters, you must strip yourself of an agenda and become natural at talking with others. Having an agenda/reason to talk to them encompasses all your weird, needy stuff, your player drills, your opinion openers, your open-ended questions – all those things designed to hide your Pick Up intentions. Most guys in this field believe Pick Up to be about tricking people, approaching unsuspecting women, slipping under a girl's radar and all sorts of deception. Having such an approach to your game will make you come across as weird and needy. The true path lies somewhere else. You need to realize you are talking to other human beings, not targets, obstacles, or "bitches." If it feels awkward to approach a girl, then you still go by the agenda: you haven't attained normalcy; you haven't grown proficient at chatting to strangers.

Why else – when I tell my students on my program to stop "picking up" and start talking to people for real – do they get their best stuff done? Their mind, stripped of outcome and results dependency, functions better. Without the result-monkey on their back, guys glide free into conversations. Without the need to control them, results happen by themselves. This apparent paradox lies at the heart of this discipline.

Approaching Without Openers

I found the best way to go about this technique to be something I call "kick the door down" rather than "knock on the door." Let me explain. Most guys approach by trying to sneak into other people's conversation with sophisticated open-ended questions, opinions, and openers. In other words, they try to slip under the radar and lock in with enticing conversation. They use a sales technique called "putting your foot in the door." Yikes! No, thank you very much. I'd rather not do that. I am not a salesman – because I have nothing to sell. You will find the "sneak-in" approach an uphill battle to get a conversation going. People will be naturally suspicious of you and you must sweat your way into making them approve of you.

Let's look at an alternative.

Sneaking In vs Barging In

When you walk in a group, you don't want to sneak in. You want to explode in with a super loud voice, Physical Game, good humour and the like. You want to rock. You want to make your presence known. Let them feel you have arrived. I call this the "momentum theory." You bring a tremendous amount of positive energy that will propel you for the next 20 minutes. Then you glide. Your interlocutors carry you on with their questions and implicit interest – just like a wind current would a glider. Those 20 minutes turn into 40 minutes, to an hour. Barging into a group as if possessed by Satan, with lots of energy, will carry you for a long time in an interaction. Most times you will only do a couple of approaches during the night. When your momentum theory is in action, short and shallow exchanges will be reduced to a minimum. With lengthier and therefore deeper exchanges you will get laid far more consistently – or retrieve solid lay leads in the form of phone numbers. The actual words that you use to start conversations – known as openers – are for the most part irrelevant, because you are going to jump straight into your own topics – like your passions. You can start with anything from: "Hi, my name is..." to: "How are you guys doing tonight?" followed by: "Guys, check this out..." And then jump into your greatest passion in life.

Most guys, out of fear of failure, go the other way. They try to sneak into the conversation by making a low-key approach and testing the waters with dubious body language, only to subliminally communicate to their group that they don't deserve to be there in the first place. They find themselves swimming against the current from the get go.

Since their interactions lack momentum they must keep forcing conversations uphill. Unable to get deep into interactions, those guys end up doing lots of groups and getting nothing. You want to avoid such frustration. You must aim to have long exchanges that will yield lays, make outs or otherwise solid leads and phone numbers.

Knee Jerk Reactions To Approaching

Through the countless approaches I myself have carried out for the past 6 years, and after watching students go at it for more than four, I have come to the conclusion that people act like mirrors. They reflect everything you give them. You make your approach friendly; they indulge you with their bonding. You behave aggressively; they turn irritable. You come along with low energy; they seem to get down too. People kick back whatever you give them. And they return it multiplied tenfold. If you give them negativity, expect doom as a payback.

On a closer look, they seem to mirror your feelings, your approach, even your body language. Not uncommon. After you have been physical with a girl for a while, she starts to reciprocate by grabbing you back. Not only her – but also her whole group. And they give it back tenfold. They seem to get into the energy you give them and multiply it by ten. By the way, the opposite is also true. You give them negativity; you get a thunderstorm back. So, beware of what you give out.

If people reflect your behaviour back, you want to give them something positive to work with. You want to walk around with a permanent but genuine smile. You must find a reason to get excited and share your excitement with people. You will find it hard to fake this. You must make it true for you.

Moreover, I also want to project a chill vibe around people because I want them to be relaxed around me. Most guys approach with outcome dependence or a desire to control others – only to succeed at freaking people out. You will find it hard to relax around people if you run around the club with a Pick Up agenda in your head. A negative attitude will self sabotage you out of your groups. People will pick up on your "weird" vibe and they will run like the wind from you. Staying easy-going around others pays extreme dividends when you aim to stabilise an interaction.

I will always remember the time I took my first live programme as a rookie student. My instructor approached a group of four girls and without warning he leaned back with his right leg against the wall like he just didn't care. Girls giggled and looked mesmerized around him while he sipped his drink through a straw. At the time it blew my mind that anyone could chill like that with strangers within minutes. Aim to relax people around you by behaving like you've got nothing to lose. To do this, you must let go of acceptance seeking from girls.

Non-Pick Up Related Conversations. Or, Just Being Social

Talking to people in a club makes you gregarious in a social situation. You must not be embarrassed or think less of yourself. You will find people in these places strike friendly conversations with each other all the time without any particular reason to do so. Unlike an office, people hang out in a club to mingle with a crowd on their down time. You must not feel awkward to do the same.

They must get with your program or otherwise exercise democracy– if they don't like you they can walk away. By initiating an interaction you don't force them to talk to you. With plenty of freedom of movement in a club they can leave anytime they see fit. Conversely if they choose to stay, they have expressed their implicit desire to know you. An added bonus in a club: you don't have to talk to people you don't like.

The Linear Model Of Attraction

Forgive me for taking you twice down memory lane. Bear with me because it will help you understand why I am so big on not seeking approval.

For you to understand my point, I need to explain the old school linear attraction formula or "linear model" as many call it. It went along the following lines, with variations depending on who was explaining or rehashing it: you "open-attract-rapport-close" ("close" meant get physical, phone number, kiss close, get her home, etc).

We could consider it a sales pitch.

It was designed to allow you to sell yourself to a girl by means of all kinds of witty, crazy, funny, enticing stories. Once you had an assurance that she was attracted to you (or your material, you never know!) you were supposed to attempt to close with her. Much like a sales pitch: make her sign on the dotted line!

Reality proved this linear pattern to be a fiction. Interactions in the field proved over and over things would not go as planned 99 percent of the time. Once again, human social exchange seems not to fit into any costume. No two gregarious intercourses are alike. It was revealed in time that interactions don't follow a linear pattern.

They never did and never will.

No matter how much Pavlov crap you bring to the table, interactions will go anywhere; chips will fall where they may. Human interactions cannot and will not fit into a mould. Once you admit that, where does this so-called "Structured Game" leave you? What is its validity – other than pleasing your mind with a feel good formula that fails in empiric terms?

> ### Reality Check
>
> *Since there is no structure to human interactions we can only follow guidelines. You should go with general ideas for action – so you have more room for manoeuvring and flexibility than with a straight-jacket-type model. With flexibility and flow being the key to your exchanges, you have a better chance at becoming good at relating to people. Rigidity must be substituted for flexibility. Swift gut action must replace logical thinking or any kind of formula.*

I realized after looking in detail at most of my lay reports (my write ups of what happened with a girl, from meet to sex) how every time I got laid there was no real structure to be found in our interactions. It seemed chaotic and things would look crazy at times with random events aligning into place to allow me to get laid- sometimes luck, other times my energy. Here, persistence and balls. There, nice and quiet rapport. None of it followed any linear structure whatsoever. Aside from being nonsensical and paranoid, a linear model reeks of the delusion of control- the need to try and enforce order in chaos. Order and solution to chaos can only be found in your head. Having said that, if we want to become "closers" we must sit in chaos and roll with the punches. I found this approach far more sane and healthy than following a structure. I also have seen the effect of this on my students, and how they flow and avoid getting stuck in their heads in a tight fitting costume with zero room for flexibility. I have taught both and I am convinced that the Self-expression Game will do the job far better than the structured, Scripted Game.

What's Closer Game?

In a nutshell: starting at the end. When I was running Scripted Game, groups would open up better when I assumed they already liked me. In other words, I seemed to function like a well oiled machine, when I was under the impression they were attracted to me from the start.

So it paid for me to imagine they were into me right off the bat, instead of having to work for the attraction with lines and stories.

Soon, I began dropping more and more lines and routines from my arsenal and I started to be more naturalistic – if you will. To the point that I dropped all of the scripted material and went with 100 percent gut instinct.

To put it in linear terms, when you do "Closer game" you are starting at the end. I mean to bypass the whole linear formula and start right at closing. No need to work for attraction when you think you already have it. The linear formula instructs: you must open, then, attract, then, rapport and then "get physical and close the deal". But, instead, you must START at "get physical and close the deal". You want to get physical from the beginning and kick off closing from step one, the opener.

In order to do this you need to ASSUME ATTRACTION. You need to think you are good enough as you are – with no dazzling story or demonstration of your "goodness". You want to be able to step into a group and think they all want you. *I know it seems too far out, but I must ask you to suspend your judgement while I teach how you can become this type of guy.*

What A Closer Does

A closer assumes attraction and behaves accordingly. A cool guy with a lot to offer, he reckons any girl will be into him if he gives her a chance. A mentality like the one I just explained will get you laid in no time.

This winning mindset has been extracted and backwards engineered from highly successful natural guys. They never think a girl will not be attracted to them. Since they feel desirable, when they see a girl they already assume they are going to hit it off. With his nonchalant behaviour the natural subliminally communicates the right vibe to make things happen. Assuming she will be into you will cut through the bullshit of attraction building. You will behave on autopilot.

How do you conduct yourself when you have detected a girl likes you? Without the stress of having to get approval – you already got it – you turn loose, you flirt, you play, you tell jokes and you regale her with the best of your personality. Naturally attractive men do the same.

Always Be Closing

A closer burns interactions to the ground. He doesn't let go until he sees the end of it. Meaning: you don't walk away at the first sign of resistance. You keep going no matter what and you stretch every interaction as far as you think it possible. Many guys ask me: "But when do I stop? Where is the boundary?" Well, there is no boundary except in your head. But for the sake of an explanation I say: "You stop when she leaves. If she is still there, she wants you."

This mentality, burning interactions to the ground, proves over and over to be the most efficient in the field. Don't give up and girls won't give up on you. Counterintuitive as they are, reference points like these will only reveal themselves after you have been in the field of practice for a while. It becomes very obvious that you will never know if a girl fancies you unless you push your exchange with her to the limit.

That's enough for now on Closer Game. I will get deeper into this when I explain Physical Game later on because there is no closing without a physical element to interactions.

Stay tuned for the next chapter, where I will teach you how to weed out your unsocial tendencies or "weird vibes" from your game, as well as how to approach with 100 percent consistency by using "self-amusement" in the field.

CHAPTER 3

On Attraction And Starting Conversations (Part 2)

*Learn How To Welcome And Conquer Token Resistance. Also:
How To Blast Through Your Comfort Zone And Approach Girls,
How To Have Fun And Much More...*

Are Girls Approached All the Time?

Yes, by lame guys.

It's very important when we approach a girl not to overlook the obvious. A girl, even mildly good looking, gets approached in a lame manner by lots of guys. For the most part by guys who are trying to get lucky on a Friday night. Girls develop default reactions to lame attacks/approaches over years of meeting guys— knee jerk reactions if you will. It behoves you not to be deceived by these reactions. Always expect a little resistance at the beginning – for girls need to weed out the insecure guys who besiege them. But! Don't be fooled! Single girls go out to meet guys.

If she had a solid relationship or a real boyfriend, she wouldn't be there unless she came as part of a group: hen, office or birthday party. Outside those aforementioned exceptions, a girl on a Friday night wants to meet a guy. Not any guy. The right kind of guy. Your average student on a live program walks out of a group giving up because his girl told him she had a boyfriend. I ask those guys: "If she has a boyfriend, why is she here alone?" Then, I send them right back to her.

Over the years I developed a rule: if her boyfriend doesn't show up, right there, I treat her as a single woman, period. I have slept with many girls who gave me the boyfriend warning at the beginning. As it turned out later, after further enquiry, the so-called boyfriend was just somebody she was seeing or sleeping with. Consider this run-of-the-mill behaviour for a woman and don't be fooled. Don't pussy out of an interaction because you find some resistance at the beginning. Instead stay strong and plough on through.

This being so important, I will make a brief stopover and explain the following concept in depth.

Token Resistance – Or Why You Want To Love Ploughing Through

When you first come to her and introduce yourself, the question: "Who the hell is this guy?" pops for a second into a girl's head. I have even recorded this momentary reaction on camera myself – yes, I have approached girls with a camera in my hand and aimed it at them. So sue me. I can pause the video at the exact point when by their facial reactions they reveal this question is going through their minds. In fact, I show it on video to my seminar students.

If you don't know what I mean, think about the last time a stranger stopped you for directions on the street. There was a split second there when you asked yourself: "Who is this guy? What does he want?" But then your mind went: "It is ok, he just needs directions." You passed a quick judgment on whether that guy was safe or not safe to talk to.

The same happens with girls. At the beginning, they make snap judgements. Those make-or-break decisions run along the lines of: "Is this guy cool or lame?" If you invest too much in their approval right off the bat, they go: "Lame!" and turn their backs on you. Sorry guys. Girls don't have much time due to the ticking of their biological clocks. Their minds, seeking to breed with an ideal male, will scope for signs of lameness and discard less-than-ideal suitors.

Token resistance, a screening mechanism for girls, develops over years of meeting guys. Programmed to detect and weed out lame males in order to breed, women test your resistance to rejection. That's why I love it when they give it to me. I see it as an opportunity to show her I am not your average Joe. I want to push through her initial wall and have a big chance at converting an apparent up-hill interaction into a lay.

Unless you get used to breaking through that kind of front you won't get laid. Most of the students I have trained to amazing success during and after programs refused to be fazed by this kind of behaviour.

Master ploughers, as I call them, even enjoy working their way through initial resistance.

> ### Reality Check
>
> *If you crave positive reactions right off the bat when you first approach (called 'approval seeking' in Game lingo), you will be pigeon holed under 'entertainer' or 'spineless' labels. In both cases girls lose interest fast. Most guys who abandon ship early, or give up on a girl too soon, do it because they don't get the reactions or approval they were looking for right away. Since girls are programmed to screen males and not give approval right away, those guys end up bouncing off girl after girl all night and getting zero results.*

Why The "Just Being Social" Mindset?

I look at my time in clubs approaching women as my socializing time. There is a time to go to your gym, a time for your friends, a time for family, and a time to get laid. In my socializing time I approach people and find out if they are cool so I can have a great time around them. The last thing in my mind is sex.

You could ask me: "But when do I get laid?"

Getting laid is a natural outcome of being social. It comes with the territory. You won't get laid unless you become social. And by social I mean being comfortable talking to new people, not being afraid of telling them about the real you. By being gregarious and applying Physical Game, you cannot help but get laid with an ever-increasing number of women.

Most guys get it wrong. For them, getting laid comes first. They thrive on it. For the most part, they are horny and they try to manipulate people, women or whoever, in order to get the outcome they desire. Excessively scared people might discover their Pick Up agenda, guys never show their real self to others.

Manipulating and trying to control the outcome of interactions will make you appear both needy and desperate. People will feel you have a Pick Up agenda. Women's interest will wane and die as soon as they sense that you seek something. In other words, trying to control other people's behaviour or scheming will only hurt you. In order to stay away from such behaviours, your sole agenda must be meeting new people and enriching your life. Sex comes as a side dish attached to your hobnobbing main course anyway.

Why You Shouldn't Hide

Most guys, because of their so-called Pick Up agenda, hide their true personalities. All their energy goes into deceiving, manipulating and wowing people with their act. I found this to be a waste of time and energy. Women, who are neither blind nor stupid, can see through you. Women have developed a high-tech radar to identify duplicity and deceitful behaviour. They can see you don't know what to say next. They can perceive you scheming and being phony to them. A professional of deceit could pull it off – but your average guy cannot.

Why all the trouble? I must advise you not to hide here. Tell them without deviation what makes you tick as a person. Even if you deem your authentic personality silly and uninteresting. I have found guys conceal genuine stuff about themselves for no reason. Far more exciting and enticing to a girl than any story they could ever fabricate to impress, their true self holds people's attention at a deeper level.

I call this process normalization. By normal, I don't mean average. I refer to the fact most guys cannot behave like themselves around girls they like.

Social anxiety– not being comfortable around people– stems from not coming to terms with being yourself. People with this problem do everything in their power to conceal their authenticity in order to get approval. Most men don't know they don't have to.

For instance, some time ago I was in my favourite salsa club in London. I danced with this Swiss girl and she proceeded to introduce me to her friend. I danced with her friend and then we all started talking and it turned out she was a cartoonist. I mentioned how I grew up watching the *Bolek and Lolek* cartoon from the Czech Republic, which was a horrible communist- era-indoctrination animation for children. She mentioned her mother was Czech and had immigrated to Switzerland. We started having a laugh at *Bolek and Lolek* and began a great conversation about cartoons. We ended up hanging out for the whole night. Phone numbers were exchanged at the end. I am in an exclusive relationship right now so there was no petting –but I am pretty sure we will hang out sometime...

What's my point? Although you might think talking about my favourite cartoon from the communist past might not entice anybody or be conversation candy, it worked. Why? Well, it was real for starters. I didn't lie. I was not afraid to admit I grew up watching propaganda for children. In other words, I was comfortable being my real self around that girl. She could see I was normal and not a lame guy trying to impress her. Being comfortable in your own reality sucks people into your reality. The opposite will just push people further away from you.

I make my favourite opener with students: "What was your favourite cartoon growing up?" Once I get an answer, I say: "Ok. Walk up to a girl and open with that. Tell them what you think about that cartoon." They go up and say: "I think X cartoon was the greatest." After that, they strike up a conversation for the next hour. Most guys cannot believe on hindsight they could start talking to a girl by using *Bambi* or *The Flintstones*.

> *Reality Check*
>
> *Don't talk about things you think they would like to hear. Rather, tell them about you. Remember you are an unknown to them and be normal. Talk about yourself and you will not run out of things to say. Show your personality without fear or judgement. Don't judge yourself. Let them judge you.*

Unlikely Worst Case Scenarios

You will find that most people act friendly and take you in as long as you don't behave like a weirdo and as long as you keep cool. No need for sophisticated strategies or tactics here. Be enthusiastic! That's about the only rule I have.

Worst-case scenarios never arise. I call this the fallacy of disasters. No doom will fall upon you. Nobody will bite your head off for talking to them. Nobody will beat you up. Guys with girls whom you approach will be super friendly for the most part, provided you talk to them in a cool way. Nobody gets into fights unless they want to.

As to people being rude to you, most people will be polite when dismissing you. Girls who don't want to talk to you will say: "We have to go the toilet," or "We are going back to our friends" and excuse themselves.

So what's your problem when approaching? Well, fear itself, fear of the unknown, fear of doing something new you haven't done before. Once you have done it and repeated it over time, approaching women becomes simple and normal. Most guys struggle with unfamiliarity. Not in the habit of approaching strangers in a club, they need time to get used to it. But after a while, fear dissolves and nightclubs stop being scary and turn into places of opportunity rather than dread.

Bank robber Willie Sutton's famous answer when asked why he robbed banks was: "Because that's where the money is." So, the reason we go to clubs is because that's where the girls are. Hundreds of them can be found in one place. Just like shooting fish in a barrel.

Why Not To Ask A Lot Of Questions

Out of sheer panic about awkward silences, guys turn to questions. Why? It doesn't take a genius to produce 20 unsolicited questions: "What's your name?" "Where are you from?" "Where do you live?" "Do you like the music here?" And so on.

It doesn't take much to understand that most people will be turned off by such talk. It's known in our trade as the 'interview style'. Instead of a normal chat, you go into a job interview mode. Because every guy does this when they don't know what to say, most girls have seen it all many times, and grown to be repelled by it. Women will just excuse themselves and leave and some might even be rude to you for boring them to death. Feeling interrogated for no reason and no crime, most will resent you. It is a no-no. As in, don't you ever.

Let's look at the alternatives.

Brilliance of Statements. Learn How Being Bold Can Change The Way You Interact With Women

A bold statement allows you to be yourself and say whatever you feel like saying around girls. I ask guys to tell me what they would like to say deep down to a girl about a particular subject. I ask them to turn their sensors off and tell me how they feel about, for example, women's shoes.

I, of course, forbid bad language and insults – just to be safe. But I want them to be honest. I one time had this guy telling me. "Women's shoes are very confusing to me." We approached girls that night by saying: "Women's shoes are confusing to me." He aced all night with that.

Most guys find it hard to stop talking after they say something bold. They feel they must explain themselves. More like, apologise for having a spine. I force them to shut up and listen to the girls. They must let the girl fill in the gaps of the conversation after saying their bold sentence. This single bold statement drill here has produced major epiphanies on day one of my live program. Guys cannot believe what happens. They express themselves honestly around a girl and the girl loves it.

> *Reality Check*
>
> *Women hate being interviewed. Instead make a lot of statements. Follow this rule of thumb: never ask girls questions before they do. Avoid the interview style. Be assertive. Instead of asking, take. Instead of questioning, affirm. Let's say you want to ask: "Where are you from?" Instead, use: "Let me guess, you are from...." And that's just a tiny example. You don't want to ask a whole lot of questions, especially at the beginning of an interaction. Use lots of sentences starting, "I want..." "I think..." "I believe..." I force my students to start conversations with statements. I try to make them more assertive from the get go. As well as reaffirming yourself, being assertive communicates you are confident around people.*

What Topics Of Conversation Should I Use Once I Am In?

First thing: I wouldn't talk of anything that doesn't amuse me. If I see a conversation going in a direction I don't like I cut her off with something like: "That's great, but check this out," and I change gears into something I enjoy like salsa dancing or Barcelona– where I used to live – or similar. Most guys have a problem with this approach because they consider it impolite. Well, being a nice guy will not get you girls. Approval seeking only will get you into try hard territory – read: most women will lose interest fast.

Once you get down to it, and by approaching lots of girls, you will find yourself talking about your personal interests and turn-ons. One student said after the first night of live program; "I have opened with girls by talking about pineapples, tap water and my country. So simple."

It's uncomplicated enough because – as you will find out after you approach hundreds of girls – what you talk about, your content, becomes irrelevant since our feelings, emotions, and general vibe account for as much as 90 percent of your success rate.

On nights you feel good, positive, enthusiastic you will float to success. On other less inspired nights, you must make it happen out of sheer muscle work. Human beings don't have the luxury of pushing a button to execute to perfection- a growth process needs to happen. Don't give yourself a hard time for it. Regardless of your level of skill, you will have nights where you tank. Get over it. Tomorrow is another day.

COACH DRILL
What's your favourite song?

Open with "my favourite song is..." Get her excited about it, sing it to her, explain it to her, and sell it. Simple as that. When you use this great conversation starter you don't need to ask her if she knows your song. Don't start with a question. Not needed. Don't set it up. Just let it rip.

However odd you might think opening a conversation with your favourite tune, it doesn't matter. You will be excited about it and she will be thrilled too. Most guys deem things like this farfetched, and not suitable for Pick Up. You will find out sooner or later that telling girls what you like and feel good about makes all the difference.

Why Expression Not Impression?

Express, not impress. I drill this into my student's heads throughout my program. Why do I make a big deal out of it? Approval seeking lies at the heart of trying to impress somebody. Just as an entertainer goes about his business of creating a good impression on his public, so a guy trying to get the appreciation of a hot girl has to juggle and act. But he neither gets paid nor has he been trained to entertain. It comes as no surprise when he bombs at his newfound career choice.

Trying to impress is self-defeating because you give your power away. Women know they have power over you in the way they respond. So they will use it. They will defer, withhold, give and take away approval as they see fit. You cannot blame them if you have given up your right to be yourself and sold it out for acceptance.

Getting approval will never get you girls – at best it will get you a friend or somebody to talk to. For the most part approval seeking in any of its forms (entertaining, being nice, telling enticing stories) will push girls away from you. Conversely, being yourself (genuine, authentic, disregarding approval, and having a self party-self expression as a whole) will put you in the driver's seat. First of all, you will be in control of yourself; secondly you will suck people into your reality ten times faster.

Approval should come from within you– at the crossroads where Pick Up as a practice meets spirituality. You must approve of your actions, life story, defects and talents. But being constrained by time and not wanting to bore you, I won't get into that topic. Let's just say you should express yourself without censorship– without the need to cherry-pick your words and opinions to get others to like you.

Impression And Outcome Dependence

In case I was not explicit enough, I will tell you yet another reason to avoid trying to impress others. When you try to get people to react in a certain way, you develop outcome dependency. In this case, you chase after a certain reaction. Your whole system gets hooked on trying to accomplish your goal of getting approval. Because you chase an outcome, people see it, and they get spooked out. At an emotional level, this translates into frustration. Every time you don't get approval you will feel worse and worse. You will spiral down into a poor mental state. This will have a domino effect on your performance.

You will then enter a vicious cycle of outcome dependence: no outcome resulting in bad mental state, and because of this bad mental state, you will accomplish no outcome. The more you fail, the worse you feel. You end up quitting and going home. Having experienced it in my own practice, on my program I focus on process, not on outcome.

Liking To Be Liked. Approval Seeking

Humans like to be liked. Most guys don't feel good unless they get approval. Therefore, guys crave approval from girls. If males don't get their taste of positive regard they will crumble from the lack of incentive. Most guys I teach feel they need to be funny when they talk to a girl. They memorize jokes or lines that will guarantee a good reaction – read approval. However, there is just one problem: when they don't get their desired laughs they feel foul. Their confidence gets shot to pieces.

This happens to people who look for assent outside themselves. Incapable of validating their own story internally, they crave other's consent for who they are. They need someone else's good will to feel good. They feel they don't deserve to feel good unless their environment gives them approbation. Much like a comedian, they need a sympathetic audience to get loose.

But Pick Up cannot be approached as a show business production. Entertainers have a hard time in this activity. Because they are doing an act they spend tremendous amounts of energy trying to get reactions out of people. Such energy could be used for getting a girl but instead it gets wasted in useless prancing. In other words, your social environment, not you, will be dictating how you feel- this is the risk when approval seeking or entertaining.

Be Aware Of "Entertainer" Mode

An entertainer works under the following assumption: "The more they like me the better I am." This type of mindset has far reaching destructive implications. If you follow this path, you will become an expert manipulator or schemer, skilled getting positive regard from people. You will devise sophisticated plans to get people to react well to you. You will spend so much time manipulating responses from women you will confuse them about your real intentions. Most will be led to think you are carrying a hidden agenda. They will get suspicious and remove their approval as fast as they gave it to you.

When you are an entertainer or in entertainer mode-you can switch into this mode at different times – if and when people treat you well you feel well; but when they don't, you get defensive. Women are very good at spotting an approval junkie and they will lose interest in you. You are nothing but another chump in a long list of guys who have tried to get into her pants by aiming to impress her.

Why Being Loud Works

Being loud will take care of everything. When I discovered that just by raising my voice I could get through any kind of resistance when approaching women, I devoted myself to going louder than loud. I took karaoke, did voice projection exercises, yelled across the street to girls. I wanted to start booming as soon as I stepped into a group and do away with any kind of resistance. I would walk into a coffee shop and talk loudly to the girl behind the counter so that the whole line could hear what I was saying. I practiced being loud everywhere I went. It became part of me.

Being loud conveys too many good things to be ignored. It shows power, authority (not to mention manliness) and gets people to trust you right away. People give you credit because, by being loud and letting everybody hear your words, you also convey you have nothing to hide. Amazingly enough, you can tell them something ridiculous, like you saw a pink elephant flying outside, and they will buy it.

Programmed to obey by society, most people submit to a loud presence. Think of your dad, your high school principal and your teachers: they all had one thing in common – they projected their voices. They had power and authority over you and they knew it. They were not afraid to be loud. When you project your voice, believe it or not, you become a powerful figure to those who listen. You become untouchable. Many times I asked myself why, without being funny but loud, girls giggle when I talked to them. They were after approval. Once you show you have power, people will smile and be nice to you. All of a sudden they want approval from you.

What's The Secret To Opening Up Big Groups?

Go in hard. Knock down the door. You don't want to sneak in or knock first. Don't ask for permission to do what you want to do. Approach them hard with lots of energy, burn your bridges as you go in and don't look back. Otherwise you will find yourself back-pedalling and leaving as soon as you get a bit of resistance.

Big groups, if you can handle them, pay off big. For the most part, not only do they contain the hottest girls in the club, but also by entering larger social packs it will make you look better in front of the rest of the club. If you can lead ever-grander groups, you will see how others, outside your group, want to talk to you too. Quality recognizes quality. Game recognizes game.

Big groups make for good training since social pressure doubles or triples when you have six or seven people looking at you, as opposed to a lazy two or three person circle. I tell my students to open big groups all the time so they get used to heightened public adversity.

What If Your Group Scatters?

Big groups in loud clubs break down into smaller groups to converse. Most of the time, you end up talking to two or three people within a larger group. Don't panic when your group divides into smaller chunks. You don't need to engage everybody. Once they all see you chatting with a small part of their circle, the rest will be willing to talk to you. Start treating your two or three people that hang on to you like a sole group. Then, you get introduced to the rest. When this happens, you are all the way in. Don't wait to be introduced though. If possible, get to meet everybody.

The Irresistible Positive Vibe

I am a huge advocate of being positive when you talk to people. It makes sense – but common sense is never common practice. However, you want to pay attention because mirroring can derail your game. Mirroring cannot be understated as a driving force in interactions. You will notice as you approach groups that people reflect your behaviour like a mirror. If you are friendly, they are friendly back. If you are negative, they are negative. If you are joyful so are they.

> *Reality Check*
>
> *Good nights out coincide with how enthusiastic you felt at the time you were practicing game. Most guys don't make the connection between their mental state and how people reflect it back to them. Feeling in a giving mood will cause your group interactions to go well.*

It pays off to bring an irresistible positive vibe with you for the simple reason that you will get it back. Be careful not to be goofy. Stay away also from people pleasing behaviours like entertainer, dancing monkey, dancing partner for the night. Remember you want to be taken seriously too. But it must be fun for you. The rest takes care of itself.

That's why I focus on – no matter how cheesy it sounds – bringing joy into their lives. I am fixed on this idea because I know the more joy I bring, the more I get back and it takes on a multiplying effect. It spirals up and I end up staying in groups for hours and picking up the girls in them.

Why Will People Take You In?

Quality recognizes quality. You go out to have fun, have a great time, and they come out for the same reason. As long as there is no weird stuff coming into your Pick Up agenda they won't have a problem talking to you.

Furthermore, by approaching them with an irresistible friendly and positive vibe you put a lot of pressure on them to do the same. People will find it difficult to be rude to a genuinely optimistic person. That's why I have no problem approaching men and women in the same group, even boyfriends and girlfriends. By bringing a friendly vibe to the guy he has no choice but to reciprocate my optimism back, or risk looking uncool in the eyes of his girlfriend.

In other words if he got defensive, he would look weak. That's why most boyfriends freeze and just stand there and watch you talk to their girlfriends without saying a single word. You will not even notice him there. By being cool you put the social pressure on them to be cool back to you. Social pressure has a paralysing effect on people.

"I Have Nothing To Say." Blaster. Open With Honest Opinion

To do this drill you must think of something mundane, like fried chicken, and come up with an honest opinion on it no matter how retarded. For best results, do it on the fly without much thought. Rule out insults, profanity and trying to get approval, and let your honest opinion be heard. The drill will not work unless you voice your honest opinion. Say whatever you feel like saying about anything.

Guaranteed to succeed in making you confident, this powerful drill can go a long way in turning you authentic in your interactions. I call it "blaster" because it creates major epiphanies in students. Since they are under the impression that in order to have success with women, they must approach with crafty, well-thought-out opening lines, guys cannot believe they can start a conversation by saying something they feel like saying. But they can and it blows their mind.

When you start, it's very important NOT to make your line into a question. It needs to be an assertive sentence. Don't set it up either like this: "I live in Newcastle, and when I come to London, I always compare the taste of Coca Cola in London with the one in Newcastle. I think Coca Cola taste better in Newcastle." No need to explain. Just say how you feel about something: "You must know Coke tastes better in New Castle." Then shut up. Let women fill in the gaps. Voice your honest opinion and wait. Never mind the awkward silence. Do it with several groups until you get the hang of it. Don't be discouraged if you fail to get positive reactions in your first attempts because you will be a bit shaky with this for a while. After a couple of approaches, you will see yourself feeling more comfortable saying something authentic to people.

Another "I Have Nothing To Say To Her" Blaster. The Zero Approval Opener

Think of the very thing about yourself that would get you the least approval from a girl. Leave sex out for obvious reasons. Try and think of a thing you would never say to a girl under any circumstance because it might embarrass you. Let's say you dance in your underwear at night when you can't sleep, or you hug a teddy bear when you go to bed. I want you to walk up to a girl and start a conversation about it. Not only that, I want you to start talking to her by saying out loud that very embarrassing piece of information. I don't want you to embellish it to make it more appealing to her by turning it into a question or a game or anything resembling entertainment or approval seeking. I want you to say as you approach: "I want you to know I pee in the shower sometimes,". "Girls, I am 24 and I still live with my parents". Or whatever; then shut up and let her fill in the blanks.

It rarely fails. It never ceases to amaze me how well women respond to a piece of honesty from a guy. In fact, with my clients, the very thing that they thought would not get any approval becomes their standard opening line. They love it. It blows their minds too that something they thought was embarrassing will get them so much approval. I keep reiterating to them not to approval seek and instead talk honestly.

This works because congruency, authenticity and being genuine attract women like honey. They don't meet a truly authentic man every day let alone in a club, where guys would say anything to get into a woman's pants. Since I force my students to be honest and authentic right from the start, a girl knows she has met somebody unique. To achieve congruency you must be truthful to yourself. Use it as a tool.

Zero Approval Seeking

On the first night of my program, I always enforce the zero approval policy. I tell my clients I don't want them to seek any approval whatsoever. The zero spinning point must be reached by letting chips fall where they may in interactions. You do your best job when you pass what I call your threshold for approval.

This zero approval zenith can be reached after a couple of hours of talking to people without caring about their opinion of you. Saying what you mean and meaning what you say will make you travel faster because you don't carry the weight of duplicity. Without the extra load of entertaining, others guys become un-reactive after a while. For some, it doesn't take long to stop caring. They arrive at their zero approval mark as little as half an hour into the night.

I don't aim to make them jerks for one night, far from it. However, trying to be liked will keep you from success. Trying to get positive regard from your girls every time will precipitate you into doom before you even start. You can get female approbation all night but not get a single girl to go home with you.

> ### COACH DRILL
>
> *Write 10 embarrassing things that you won't ever tell a girl about yourself. Then make it a point to walk up to girls and start a conversation with them. Keep reminding yourself that you don't have to be different or interesting to talk to a girl.*

100 Percent Expression Point. Your Good Energy Vibe

I find this to be the golden state of mind. I teach guys to express, not impress. I hammer this mantra throughout my program. I repeat this piece of knowledge over and over and I explain it in different ways as my students do approach after approach. I know some of them will try to impress girls, by saying all kinds of things that would get a girl's attention – like funny stories, or boasting about their travels. They invest in seeking approval, which turns them into entertainers.

> **Reality Check**
>
> *Attention seeking and/or approval seeking will deplete energy levels. They are both controlling behaviours requiring a lot of energy on your side to keep up. You will feel drained and bummed out very early because you are focusing on things outside your control, like attention or approval. It is up to people to give you attention and approval not you. You will do better when you stay focused on things you can control (like your attitude, approaching, having fun, etc.) and forget about other people's behaviours.*

As our night progresses in the club and I keep repeating my mantra (express, not impress), my students drop trying to impress and instead they start expressing themselves more and more. Then, with further churning of the cream, they arrive at a point in the night where they are 100 percent congruent with what they are saying. With no duplicity or manipulation in their interactions, they are 100 percent indifferent to people's reactions.

I call this mental state, *100 percent expression point.*

And you will know it when you get there because the quality of your interactions will change. They will feel effortless. It will seem like everybody wants to be around you because you are not emitting needy vibes or duplicity. You are just being yourself around people – telling personal stories, your real passions in life, and at times embarrassing things about yourself like "I have a hairy back!" and so on. You have courage, congruency, positivity and even kindness in you. You become a people magnet without trying!

For some people, this takes two hours, for others just minutes. It depends on the person and how committed you are to getting to that point. There are some, a minority, for whom this takes days to understand. I start teaching this on Friday and they get it by Sunday. But they get it. Not at a logical level, but at an emotional level. They feel it in their body, They are congruent with who they are when interacting with females, and that makes all the difference. All of a sudden a new world of opportunities opens up for them. They have dropped a big load from their shoulders. They feel lighter, faster and effective. They have to impress no more. Though this might sound like a fairy tale story, and though you might be inclined to disbelieve, students go through this weekend-in, weekend-out in my programs. Over the years, it has become a huge part of what I do. Not incantations, but real-life, nose-to-the-grindstone work.

Comfort Zone Blaster

I have another range of drills I call comfort zone blasters. I designed them to get guys out of their comfort zones.

Built to make guys break through their fear of stepping out of their ego- protecting cocoons, the radical nature of these drills will make you so uncomfortable everything else will look easy. They are the equivalent of running stark naked in the middle of a football field on a Champions League Final. Maybe that's a little exaggerated, but it will be so uncomfortable you won't worry about ridicule ever again.

I use the following comfort zone blaster on my live program: stand in front of your girl, stare at her, say nothing and start waving your hands like a five-year-old. Imagine you are having a conversation with her. Imagine she must guess what you are saying. Let's say you want to say to her: "I love London in spring". You must use your body to express this idea without using words. Nothing works better than miming your way out of your head and put you in a playful and amusing mind frame. Girls love it. Try it.

I have given most of the material you need to open and start a conversation with a girl, which can be an ordeal for your average male. However, starting conversations alone will not get you laid. You need a stronger and far more powerful tool. You need Physical Game. It makes the difference between the winners and the losers in the Friday night marathon.

Now if you are ready, I will show you what Physical Game can do for you and how it can change your sex life. So stay tuned for the mind-blowing effects of these techniques, don't hang up now, read on...

Part Three
Getting Physical

CHAPTER 4

The Benefits Of Physical Game

How Getting Physical Can Save You...
Learn Some Of The Beautiful Things PG Will Do For You

The Fast Lane

As a shortcut to sex, PG (Physical Game) can flip a girl's emotions in your favour. Those favourable emotions can be exploited with the different closing tactics I am going to give you, in order to make you dangerous out there. Nothing speaks louder than leading a girl physically. It can be considered your bridge, your missing link, and your key to tapping into a girl's emotions. Its crushing power in breaking through a girl's defences compares to that of a nuclear weapon in warfare.

Having such power leads to choice in your sexual life. Power to come into a club and know deep inside you can choose a girl you like and not get stuck with what you can get. If you apply Physical Game hard over the course of a night with every girl you run into, there will be a number of girls who will pop – meaning they will form a strong interest in you and you will stand a good chance to get laid with them.

Your "pop window" will not be open forever. When a girl pops, you have a limited time to close your deal. You need to make a decision fast about whether you want her or not. As an average – and I am not afraid to give numbers here – you will have two to three girls a night, provided you exert PG with all girls you meet. You need to make your choice. We call this scenario a master's problem. Masters have quality problems or decisions to make that are very different from those of a newbie. You want to have a master's headaches – such as dealing with extraction logistics, hot-or-not girl picks, group cock-blockery and jealous boyfriends.

Use Instant Attraction

The more you deploy hardcore PG, and see girls mesmerized, the more you will develop confidence. This can have a snowball effect on your game. The more confidence you have, the more and harder you exert PG, the more girls you attract on any given night. The more pop windows to act on or choose from, the more girls you get. It sounds like a numbers game, but (quite the contrary) you will find it comes down to self-confidence.

How far are you willing to go with this? How many mistakes are you willing to make? Remember, you want to get through your 2000 rookie mistakes as soon as possible, so you can move on to your 5000 master mistakes. You want to fail all the time, large and deep, so you can get as much experience as possible under your belt. Repeated exposure to errors creates the fertile ground where self-reliance grows.

Every time you employ PG, you play to the female's mating brain chemistry. You will see them giggling, attracted or telling you off. You need to get over the ones who don't like you and capitalize on those who pop. In doing this, you will have plenty to choose from every night. Soon enough, after intimate intercourse with multiple partners, you will cease to be horny and will start screening for sex. You will be on your master's quest to meet with your ideal girl(s). You will find this task, hard and requiring patience. Be that as it may, you want to be playing at this level, a master's level.

Why We Fear Taking The Leap To PG

When in harm's way, with real danger, we all feel justified fear, Psychological fear, on the other hand, is a latent unjustified fear. It tells us "I am afraid if/when x, y, z happens." In the absence of real danger we walk around in fear "just in case." We live in dread – no matter if x, y, z never materialize. With no real immediate threat, we fear what the future might bring. Taking into account the fact that no one can predict the future, we can safely say we are frightened of the unknown– what *might* happen vs. what is happening here and now.

This applies to the game at all levels of skill. Guys who never completed a program before are afraid that when they approach girls/ guys will do x, y, z. But x, y, z never materialize. For example, I have seen guys on program afraid to approach a mixed group (guy/girl groups), and then surprised to find out they are the easiest.

Guys panic at the idea the guy in the group will detect and blow the whistle on his Pick Up agenda, or he will be pissed off and beat him up or tell him off. No such thing ever happens and the student has an epiphany. Of course, to have such a realization, the student needs to be willing to go through with the experience of approaching a mixed gender group, and not back down. Psychological irrational fear at more advanced levels can be seen when guys don't go for the kiss because of the risk of losing their girl. But, when they try and close every girl, and they end up making out with three or four girls a night, their fear of losing subsides. They open their eyes to a new world of possibilities.

Furthermore, anxiety manifests itself as avoidance in advanced guys when they need a perfect situation for picking up a girl. "A perfect group" as we call it. They end up selecting groups in the club, losing precious time, and their mental state in the process. Ridden by the fear of failure, they need assurance of an outcome to take the leap.

Yet with zero outcome dependence you must step into the unknown and approach every group. Instead of a futile memorization of your driving manual, you must get behind your wheel and face traffic. It's scary at first, but after a little time you just don't even notice the dangers on the road. You have conquered the unknown in driving terms...

Why Do You Get Bogus Phone Numbers When You Only Use Verbal Game?

Bogus phone numbers happen when a guy talks to a girl and gets her number but she won't reciprocate attempts to contact her. If that guy is you, you get frustrated and start thinking you suck, or you are not attractive, or cannot get hot women, etc. Most males, I must add, coming from an unsuccessful background with women, will rush to such conclusions without a blink. They even refuse to look at cold hard facts and just assume they suck.

I remember my first approach in this game when I got a number. I will never forget her – because I had to muster the courage to approach a huge group of girls. Some way, somehow, I managed to talk to her and using some line I got from the internet. I tricked her into giving me her email and phone number. Our interaction lasted less than 10 minutes. I was on top of the world. It thought I was smooth and got excited.

Next day, we set up a meet in a coffee shop by text. She cancelled one hour before the meet. I was so frustrated and angry that I lashed back with some hate phone texting – telling her how she would not stick to her word and similar. But complaining about a woman changing her mind is as insane as complaining about the weather in London.

However, look at the facts. It was a 10-minute interaction. Other than introducing ourselves, we talked of nothing in particular. I was invisible to her. In such a shallow interaction – as we call them in the dating industry– she couldn't get to know me. Getting nothing comes at no surprise if you look at the cold hard facts. I had no time to tell her about myself, and she had no time to tell me about herself. We parted complete strangers. It is only natural she would balk at seeing me again.

Your other typical example is the "friend zone", as we call it. The guy approaches a girl and does nothing but friendly conversation. This goes on for a while until he runs out of things to say and exhausts her patience.

For most guys, talking is their only tool. Since he is unable to stir anything sexual in a female your average Joe ends up chatting.

Without a sexual component to your interaction, she considers you another friendly guy, but not a potential suitor for sex. She won't answer your calls. One thing women will not do is waste their time. Most women want to create a family or start a relationship because of the ticking of their biological clock. A hot girl seeks somebody with breeding potential.

You want to put plentiful and hardcore PG on all your interactions as a way of ensuring a sexual component to your exchanges. I want her to make a swift decision as to whether she wants me or not. I want her to shit or get off the pot: I don't want to waste my precious time. I want to lose a lot of girls – but, for every girl I lose, I take a risk and my confidence grows. In the process I end up with lots of girls because of increased risk taking.

More choices equals better quality of life.

Welcome To Effortless Opening

You rack your brain for something to talk about. But the content of your conversation becomes secondary or irrelevant. As a direct consequence of PG, your girls start interrogating you. They have never met such a confident guy before so it stirs their interest. So you stop worrying about what to say next.

The power of PG will enable you to circumvent your talking issue. There's no need to say anything clever, interesting or even remotely impressive.

The momentum you carry when you apply physical game will propel you way past your opening sentence into your next 20 to 30 minutes without pushing it. By utilizing what I call "Effortless Opening", you will avoid those try hard vibes most guys reek of when they start talking to a girl. In other words, you will glide into conversations.

Women Submit, Men Assert

Looking at pictures of guys being physical, you notice how women's body language changes. It turns compliant, submissive, if you will. They all seem to say: "I will do what you say." By asserting yourself over her with your physicality, you turn the tables on her.

Women submit to a strong physical guy. But you must execute. Assertiveness has a way of communicating you are the type of guy who gets what he wants. PG tells your girl you are a potential sexual partner right off the bat. Women surrender to you if you are firm and confident enough.

Most guys ask me if they should spell it out for a girl— as if they must verbalize, "I want you" or, "I like you"' to state their intentions and so avoid the ever dreaded friend zone. No need if you don't feel like it. PG speaks for you with no mixed signals: by being physical you make a point not only that you want her — but that you are going to get her.

Consistency And Speed When You Start A Conversation

Verbal skills added to the physical component get the job done faster and more efficiently. I even have tried opening without a verbal component. Just being physical breaks groups wide open for you. You must find a way to introduce yourself and shake hands and hug all the girls in the group straightaway and break the physical ice (if you will).

I do this when I run my programs in places where I don't speak the language like Eastern Europe, Brazil, and the Middle East. I know I cannot be witty or smart or funny. It won't work; they won't pick it up. So I always resort to physical game as a lifesaver. I've got laid in all the above places – and I relied on Physical Game every time.

Physical Game cuts like a knife through butter. It will blast through any verbal shortcomings you might have – like being shy or introverted. If you make a habit of using it, you will see girls taking an interest in you. You won't have to talk so much after a girl likes you. That's the beauty of it. Talking becomes secondary. You won't think of having to think of something to say as an obstacle anymore.

Prevent Drag-Aways

As a bonus you will see a significant reduction in those hated drag-aways. For example, you are talking to a chick and everything is going fine and out of nowhere comes her friend and drags her away from you. It happens countless times – and it bums you every time.

It won't occur much after you get physical because you start to look like a part of her peer group. Since you look like you are hitting it off with your girl, her group will not interfere. In fact, they might even encourage your girl to stay with you if she happens to be single.

It sounds too good to be true, I know. Well, it happens weekend in weekend out on my programs.

However, I have kept you in the dark about yet another juicy side effect of PG on surrounding people– random guys won't come into your group. They reckon that since you and your girl look like a couple they don't have a chance; so they won't approach your girl or your group. Most guys would give up as soon as they see a stronger male presence. That's exactly what you will be conveying. A dominant alpha male vibe will ensue when you use PG. So much so that other guys won't risk coming in to try to steal your girl when it looks like she fancies you. They don't want to waste their time and will move on to easier prey.

Most Dominant Presence In The Room

That's right. You want to look like you are the most dominant guy in the room. Not only will other guys back off, but also other girls you haven't touched yet will be looking forward to getting a piece of you. When you start dominating on a physical level, it looks from the outside like you are hooked up with those girls or you are at least part of the group. They think you are super social and cool. Everybody will want to know you.

You will be able to approach other groups in the same room and start a conversation without fear of being told off. How could they tell you off? They just saw you hitting it off with a group of girls. Most guys would like to have you on their side to Pick Up girls or will admire you – to say the least. Most girls, who see you in action, will want to know if you are a potential suitor for sex or relationship. There is no down side.

The more girls you lead physically, the better you get at it and as a result you will gain real confidence around females. Your leading skills will sharpen and you will be able to flip a girl's emotions faster. As a result, you will lose all your fear of being rejected.

Easier And Faster Isolation

A decisive physical lead will yield easier and faster isolation. You will be one-on-one with many girls as a result of your leading skills. Girls won't object to following you around the club to the dance floor, to a quiet spot, or similar... Getting *mano-a-mano* will become your second nature. You will have her peer group's approval too, since you look like you are hitting it off with her. In other words, women will find it hard to say no to you.

Less Is More: Longer And Fewer Groups Per Night

I am used to getting guys on my program who have been working on their skills for some time, even years. They are in the habit of doing 20-30 groups a night. Some of their usual sticking points are ejecting too early, reactiveness (uneasy) to the first signs of resistance, and a lack of solid internals.

However, we end up doing only three or four only on our first night. We stay for an average of an hour per group. They end up hooking up with two of the four. On the second night of the program, we do some more groups, improving to the point that they look like they can extract girls from any of the groups they approach.

Doing Less To Gain More

As you make progress in PG you will do less leg work, fewer groups – and hook up more. Less activity with more yield indicates solid game. It means you are doing it without effort. You are on your way to becoming a natural as you align your inner self with the principles of the game.

Learning Physical Game will help you reduce and eliminate one of your most annoying and frustrating bad habits in this area: bouncing off, doing a lot of groups and getting zero results. Out of the bad habit of only applying verbal game without a sexual component most approaches have no depth, so guys just ping-pong off from group to group at the first sign of resistance. They refuse to stick around. They end up doing a lot work with no yield.

PG will go a long way towards helping to solve those issues.

Learn How To Dish It Out To Guys Too

PG can be used on guys too. I endorse it. Apart from a strong handshake as you walk into your group, you can also plant your hand on a guy's shoulder and you will see how guys turn friendly or passive.

There are other more radical things you could do: like rapping him with your hand on his chest or back like you would a team-mate after scoring a winning goal. Every one of these things executed with ease will neutralize any kind of resistance he might give to you coming into the group. I can also recommend high-fiving for any reason mixed with a natural friendly vibe.

Eclipsing Guys

You coming in strong with PG will eclipse guys on the spot. Once they see how physical you are with your women, guys freeze. This paralyzing effect can be seen in my demo videos when I show them to my students the day after their first night on the program. Unaware of eclipsing a guy, your average student doesn't believe it until I show him the sneak video I made of him with my digital camera. Those videos show my students coming into a group, befriending everybody and then ignoring the guy while talking to his girls.

Guys have two default behaviours when they see a strong physical male presence. Either they stand there and do nothing (the boyfriend just looks at you vindictively, but refuses to interfere as you chat with his girlfriend); or they just go away and you don't see them again. Standing their ground against a dominant presence doesn't appeal to them.

Contrary to popular belief, most guys in a group are NOT PART of the group. They are guys your girls just met in the club. As soon as they see you coming in, they disappear in a hurry because they would rather move to a group with less competition. You may be tempted to think of the guy in the group as a boyfriend, but he might not be. But remember you also look like a boyfriend when you apply PG on girls. For an outsider, as you exert PG, it looks like you either know her really well or you are her boyfriend.

Mission Impossible

There are girls who are going to give you an inordinate amount of resistance when you approach them. These are hard groups to crack. So, by being physical you can open those seemingly impossible groups. As you go in with PG, you realize how their gloves go down as you plough through. For example, I will teach you how to grab her hand and spin her in order to dissipate her bad emotions.

Not only that, you will learn how to approach impossible situations like a guy and a girl making out on the dance floor. I do these "impossible mission" drills on my programs, and more than once I have seen my student pulling a girl away who was kissing another guy on the dance floor. It catches him off guard and the guy has no reaction time and loses his girl to my student.

You will be able to pull off those things and more if you learn your mindsets and techniques I will be teaching you next.

CHAPTER 5
Why We Don't Get Physical

*Learn All The Fears That Prevent You From Getting What You Want –
And How To Deal With Them*

What Are Learned Behaviours?

Before I get deeper into why guys in general refuse to get physical with women, I want to shed some light on learned behaviours. I am referring to those things that we do or don't do out of habit – and how they are learned and cemented with repetition.

By teaching you how behaviours are learned, we can address the issue of why men don't get physical with a little more clarity. For example, if you are used to going to a club to lean by the bar all night and not approach women, then you must know you won't get rid of this behaviour without a fight. Most learned behaviours die hard. After a lifetime of being a spectator, it will be a thorn in your flesh to show up in a club and approach the first girl you see, let alone get physical with her from the get-go. Your learned behaviours will resist your new initiatives.

Homeostasis

This resistance has a name: homeostasis, the unwillingness of any system to upset balance – balance being whatever you got into a habit of doing. Every cell in your body rebels and stops you dead when you try to break through with something new. It works similarly to a thermostat. A thermostat operates on a feedback loop and it acts as the guardian of change. When the temperature rises or goes below your set levels your thermostat activates, bringing back balance. With thousands of thermostats controlling different functions in our body, acting as gatekeepers of mutability, we fight against unseen forces.

While keeping the status quo, your thermostat doesn't know if change will be good or bad for you. It doesn't care. As the keeper of variability gets activated, it leaves you with resistance and merciless paralysis.

It's like going on a diet, failing and then experiencing a swift pull back into old eating habits. Our diet might make us healthier, but we find ourselves eating the wrong kind of food despite our best intentions. Most people who start diets end up giving up after two weeks. Thermostats work on overdrive and people find themselves going back to their usual burgers and fries.

The same thing happens to us when we try to implement new behaviours with regard to women. We end up sliding back to old behaviours. Despite our commitment to talk to women, we find ourselves leaning by the bar and not approaching. Or we talk instead of getting physical. We stray from our initial goals. With too much resistance to change and do uncomfortable things, we enter our comfort zone, the silent killer of game.

To overcome resistance to change, you must commit to a process of readjusting the thermostats. We need to reset your thermostat to new and improved settings and battle to keep them there. With time, effort, and repetition, these new levels become your new comfort zone.

Childhood Messages And Behaviours

Some things happen in most males' childhoods that go unnoticed or never get the rightful attention they deserve in this game. For example, how many times were you told, "Don't hit a girl," "Be nice to girls," etc.? These messages found their way into our psyche. As those ideas became part of our male identity, we don't notice them anymore. They seem to take a life of their own.

Maybe you pulled a girl's hair in grade school and your teacher reprimanded you; or your mother told you to be nice to your sister. They were all benign messages to correct your behaviour, but you were at a very tender age, an age where you learn things at a tremendous speed. Like people say, a child's mind resembles a blank canvas: you can write anything on it.

However, contrary to societal maxims, when you step into a club you will witness how the very guys who grab, spin, and pull girls around, in a seemingly aggressive manner, seem to get all the women. Most of those guys don't have those beliefs of "treat them nice." They act as if women are their toys. However, you must not misinterpret this as harassing. Girls love the physical touch of a confident guy. They welcome it. Those guys are leading girls physically, taking the initiative, running huge risks of being rejected. And that gets the job done.

Conversely, the nice guys seem to lurk by the bar, talk to friends, not approach, and get nothing. They go home alone. By the way, this has nothing to do with nice guys finish last. It has more to do with guys who don't lead, don't get laid. Be aware of your beliefs about females—especially those you acquired during childhood (your most vulnerable time) – because they will get in the way of getting physical.

Cultural Issues And Their Impact On Physical Game: Physically Distant Cultures

Fortunately for me, I come from a Hispanic background where people kiss, hold each other and hug all the time. However, I have taught around the world, including the Middle East, and I have discovered some cultures have more resistance to getting physical than others. In the US, for instance, they have all these worries of sexual harassment in the office. They also keep their distance in social situations. Not a big deal if you understand the student's mindset. By spotting these cultural differences, you can strive to change them when they walk up to a girl. For example, I instruct students to cut the space between themselves and the girls right away, regardless of the country I am in.

Invade her personal space if you must.

But I think the worst cases can be blamed on family background. Since every family stands alone as a cultural unit with its values and rules, it makes for a harder shell to break than a country's culture.

Family idiosyncrasy runs deeper in a guy's psyche than his country's customs. In some families, members don't show approval to each other in the form of touching. Guys who grow up in these conditions have a harder time with unjustified physical contact. To initiate any type of physicality with a female, they need a compelling reason to do it – in the shape of approval on the side of a girl.

You might want to think of your own family idiosyncrasy and see how it affects your game today. Then, you must make the necessary adjustments as suggested in this book. If you come from such a family background, with little or no bodily contact, you will find a great deal of resistance in you to carry out your different tactics and techniques being taught here.

You must not fear sexual harassment for grabbing a girl in a club. You can get away with all you want there, because nobody is going to sue you for trying to make out with a girl. A club is a playground, where rules about physical distance don't apply. For if there were too many rules to bow to, most people wouldn't go to clubs. It wouldn't be fun.

What Is Too Much Game?

First of all, too much game equals too much talking. Too much verbalizing – with little or no physical action. Talk forever and bore your girl forever. Most guys live under the impression that they can convince a girl verbally to go home with them. It has been tried. Without much success I might add.

If you talk to a girl for half an hour without any physical game, you will see her turning her head and looking for excitement elsewhere. What's the point of talking to a guy in a club? Make a friend? She already has a lot of friends. You will be lucky if her friends don't come to her rescue. If girls in her group see her getting bored with you, they will come and take her away from you with an excuse. You will have plenty of those so-called drag-aways if you limit yourself to talking.

As a result of too much talking, no physical lead happens. If you don't lead, you won't get a girl. She needs to see you moving her around, taking the initiative, ploughing through her resistance. A vacuum in leadership happens when you only talk. She will fill such a vacuum. She will either leave or take you back to her friends and start moving you around the venue. As you follow her, you will not be leading and thus lose your initiative. The girl's interest in you will wane and die. You will lose your status as a potential suitor for sex.

Why Do You Fear Losing The Girl?

Your fear of losing your girl will surface on occasions. Let's say you have been talking to her for a while and you quite like her. Your fear of her interest ebbing away if you get physical paralyses you. This trepidation about sacrificing one girl blinds you from the fact there are enough girls to go around – so why all your effort in keeping this one?

Scarcity mentality – not enough girls to go around – should be substituted with an abundance mentality. Dropping one girl makes no difference in the ocean of single girls around the club to pick from. Don't let insufficiency rule your game. Become a closer by losing girls because you did something, not because you didn't try. "Not now" makes for the worst mantra in the game.

Why Do We Fear Rejection When Being Physical?

Fear of rejection drives most men. Guys enter the game with the hope that, after serious study, no girl ever will reject them again. They scheme and learn every Pick Up tactic out there to prevent the inevitable: being rejected.

Their fear has to do with being stereotyped as your average horny guy in a club trying to get lucky. But a crowd in a club minds its own business and aims to have fun rather than blowing the whistle on sexually deprived men. Yet, the paralysing effect of your fear of collective rejection renders you unable to escalate physically.

Players will still be rejected long after getting good at the game. The difference is that they won't care about it anymore. Plus, getting a cold shoulder indicates you are pushing interactions to the limit. It is a healthy sign. Sooner rather than later your efforts will be rewarded with a girl.

On the other hand, most girls don't reject you. They reject your behaviour. Girls who dismiss you never had time to meet the real you. How can they be discarding you as a person? Not you, but the way you approach sabotages your best efforts. You must be doing something wrong when you start a conversation and they rebuff you. So, don't take it personally. Change the way you approach. Sometimes a small fix like upping your energy levels when you start your conversation with your girl goes a long way.

Furthermore, in this game most rejections are temporary ones. Most girls mean to say to you "not now" or "not ready yet". But most guys give up too soon and without a serious try. They don't follow through and consequently they miss opportunities to get laid. If a girl dodges your kiss close, act normal, and try it again. How many times? As long as she keeps on talking to you. A woman cannot say "no" more than three times. Keep going.

Who is The Perfectionist?

To err is a weakness – or so goes the mantra of the perfectionist. In the futile quest for perfection, you don't risk anything because you don't try anything. Without a big dose of trial and error, you can't learn anything new, and so most of those guys end up stalling their progress. They don't up their game and they finish last, without getting laid at all. Guys don't want their weaknesses exposed.

The result of a strict upbringing, where fallibility is frowned upon, the fear of failure rears its ugly head when it comes time to approach women. Households that do not tolerate wrong doing breed children who refrain from taking risks. Many parents teach their kids to avoid blunders at all cost. However, it takes a strong and healthy ego to tolerate botch-ups. But, if you can take disappointments, your game will soar. Also, errors are a sign that you are pushing your boundaries. You must welcome mistakes if you are serious about getting laid.

Finding Your Own Style

Beware of guys who don't make mistakes because they do not push interactions hard enough. You want to go over your rookie mistakes as soon as possible and start mingling like a master. In this journey, from rookie to master one thing will remain constant: errors. We learn from experience. And experience means trial and error. Go out and try it, see if it works, and do it again.

Don't back down if it doesn't work on your first try– you must repeat and learn. That's the style of the serious player. Why? Because what works for me might not work for you – and vice versa. I can't get away with things other guys do; and the same applies to them when they try my stuff. Those things that are unique to yourself will be found in the course of your practice.

Let me give you an example. Some time ago, I used to approach girls by saying: "Would you like to grab my ass?" Then I would grab their hand and put it on my ass. I was body building at the time and my body was in top shape. Most girls found it amusing to reach and slap my behind. I used to boast that I could open with my ass. At the time, it was an amusing thing to do for me. I have grown out of that one and I don't do that anymore. One thing though, I would not teach my students to open like that. It was too personal and I couldn't get them into the amusing mind frame necessary to carry out that opener. It was mine.

You can only grow in the game through mishaps. Rather than seeing them as defects, embrace, assimilate, and learn from them. Fear of making mistakes must be replaced with empiricism.

When She Has More Value Than Me

We call this problem "girl-is-hotter-than-me" syndrome. When most guys spot a girl who is out of their league – more beautiful than any girl they have had before – they freeze. Now, as they walk up to her, it becomes an impossible mission to get physical. You notice that they stand far away from the girl as they speak to her. Conversation runs out and they succeed only at making the girl uncomfortable.

Thinking "The girl is better..." causes your mind to go blank. Alternatively, we also call this "putting her on a pedestal." Guys start to show a behaviour that subliminally communicates to a girl that they don't deserve her. Attractive girls are way too familiar with this type of male aberration and it causes them to lose interest.

The scarcity mentality (not enough girls to go around), furthermore, helps create this attitude where you put girls on a pedestal. Guys think a hot girl comes once every 100 years – like a comet. They can't bear the thought of losing all that value. They won't take risks. As a result, they don't get to eat pie.

Fear Complicates Everything

Without fear, approaching becomes simpler. Apprehension separates the winners from the losers in this game. Once you become proficient at walking up to women on a regular basis, you will see a huge jump in results. For that jump to happen, second thoughts must be eliminated. Dread in all its forms – of rejection, of the unknown, of making mistakes – stops you today. Once you approach and you find it harmless, you will become bolder and take more risks. You will therefore up your ante and results will start to pile up.

When we finish approaching girls for the night on my live program I ask my standard feedback question: "What did you learn?" Students' answers go along the lines of: "I can approach now. What's next?" By "next," they mean how do I get her to go home with me?

I love to hear this because once fear of approaching women subsides I can start getting deeper into "how to get laid" territory.

Now that we have identified the most important causes of why we don't get physical, let's move on to how to do it for real. In the next chapter, I plan to get deeper into how fast we should get physical and how to do it.

CHAPTER 6

The How-To's

Learn Your Techniques:
The Very Things You Need To Do To Get Physical With A Girl Fast.
Here I Will Also Disclose What Makes People Excel At Anything And
Become Masters At Any Skill – And How That Applies To Pick Up.

On Becoming a Physical Guy

Many people who are already good at this will tell you the same thing: "It is not about the tactics and techniques" and they are right.

I want to warn you about becoming a technique addict or collector. Those people never become good at this game. Technique collectors end up just doing that: gathering information, but failing to take action.

Simplicity must rule. Less is more. I used to go in the clubs with one idea or piece of the game to practice. Once I exhausted it, I would move to something else and so on. For example, I remember training to pull girls out of clubs by trying to get every girl I met to come with me. I did that for a month. I ended up pulling many girls home that way and learning to lead in the process. I practiced the same piece until I mastered it.

I will explain the how-to's of Physical Game, but in no way will they replace core confidence – confidence in yourself. Your techniques should be your wrapping, but in no way they are your main package. I have seen plenty of guys fail at trying to get good at technique. Technique alone doesn't make a good player because communicating with other humans goes beyond the realm of craft.

When you learn something, you must become something. You must turn into a physical guy in your interactions with women. You want to be friendly and touchy so your moves don't come across as horniness, but a genuine expression of yourself. It should come naturally to you to high-five/hold hands/hug women within minutes of meeting them –

sometimes seconds. Physical Game techniques are not there to make you instantly successful, but to allow you to reinvent yourself as a physical guy.

Which takes me to my next point:

What Is Instant Gratification?

You can define instant gratification as looking for a quick fix or climactic experience all the time in order to make you feel better. Most guys want results now. In this pursuit of instant thrills, they miss the big picture. They want to walk into a club and seduce girls within their first 10 minutes of cold approaching. If that doesn't happen, they get blown off course. They start looking for reasons why they are not successful. They end up either blaming themselves or their environment. Frustration sets in.

Both quick fixes and instant climaxes are rare. Because of the unpredictable nature of this game, you will be frustrated and quit early if you are looking for something easy and fast. Moreover, if you are you incapable of learning from your own mistakes, without empiric experience of trial and error, you will be thrown away from your master's curve onto a succession of plateaus without many climactic rises.

According to George Leonard in his insightful book *Mastery*, climaxes are few and far between when you learn any skill, be it badminton, hand-weaving or Pick Up. In a skill learning curve, you encounter mostly plateaus (defined as extended periods of time where nothing happens). But you must keep practicing anyway in order to get to the next level.

Instant gratification goes against the principles of mastery in that it presumes success at learning by piling up of climax upon climax in TV commercial fashion. Frustration and hard work play no part in it. Instant gratification misleads your thinking and without climactic experiences your progress halts. However, plateaus represent the threshold of good things to come. They announce you are on the way to the next level.

Delaying Gratification

Unless you are able to delay gratification, you will be inconsistent in practice. By trying to get quick results without long-term commitment you will be thwarted. Beginners must refuse to grade their progress on a nightly basis and put it off for a month. Procrastinating has its place in the game.

Saddled with outcome dependence, most people would always evaluate themselves down instead of up. It's easier to spot loopholes than good points. So, by delaying your evaluation until the end of the month, you ensure you are not in the business of chasing after a mirage.

Delaying gratification also helps you to learn from experience. By not being focused on outcomes you can switch your attention to process and feedback from direct experience. You become less rigid when you are approaching women and flexibility plays a key role. You must nourish a learning attitude towards your practice.

Be Happy With Baby Steps!

You novices need to be happy with small progress and keep positive and uplifted throughout the learning ordeal. For this to happen you need to be thrilled with baby steps or tiny increments. Being able to narrow your focus on the small positive things plays a large role in keeping your energy up and staying upbeat.

Most people are unwilling to take small steps or walk like a turtle for a while. "It is not enough," they say. "At this speed I would never get anywhere." As a consequence of this rebellion against process, they get paralysed. They don't take any action because they can't find a shortcut. However, slow and steady works in this game. Breaking a big task down into simple, do-able steps can transform you into a champion.

Let's say, for example, you haven't been able to approach a single girl in your entire life, let alone hook up with a woman in a club. Then on your first night ever approaching you get mixed reactions, but no desired outcome was achieved. All the same, you need to pat yourself on the back and get excited. First of all, you broke through your fear of approaching– a huge step for a newbie. Refuse to behave like most guys, who would focus on the mixed reaction side of the deal. Don't ask yourself irrelevant questions like: "What did I do wrong for those girls to reject me?" But remember, you approach first and foremost to break through your fear of approaching. And that's what you did. Be happy with baby steps.

But How Do We Learn?

It took me a while to figure this one out. I must admit I was clueless until I found a little book called *Mastery* written by George Leonard. It was eye opening to me to find out my students learned faster and better once they knew how they learn.

In his book, George Leonard profiles three major learning types: the Dabbler, the Obsessive and the Hacker. The author had years of teaching experience under his belt. (Literally, he was an Aikido instructor-before he came up with these profiles.) We all fall into these three categories. By knowing how we learn we can increase our speed of learning. I have had so much success teaching this that I was compelled to share it in this book.

Let's break the major learning styles down.

If you are a run-of-the-mill Dabbler, you will practice a new skill for the novelty of it. Then, your initial enthusiasm wanes and dies when you realise it takes some extended repetitive experience to get yourself to a master level. The hard work gets you bored and you want to move on to a new activity. This "new" activity or sport could be different but you will forever remain within the same learning pattern and the same cycle will be repeated. Dabblers like to start things but never finish them. They have no follow through capacity. Dabblers have long resumes but no steady job.

The typical Dabbler reads a book or watches a DVD on Pick Up and he becomes excited and starts to talk about it with friends. Then he goes out a couple of days on a weekend. After he receives a couple of rejections, he goes home and shrinks from further action. He quits the game because he doesn't like being rejected. He wants things to be fun all the time. Approval ranks high for a Dabbler – who aims to feel good about himself all the time. He has low tolerance for disapproval from females.

The Obsessive, conversely, wants to see immediate mind blowing results. He starts training and wants to beat the instructor after the first lesson. When he finds out that he can't, he gets frustrated. He asks questions along the lines of: "How long before I can get good at this?" He practices hard, but disappointment sets in as soon as he finds he is incapable of quick improvement.

I have seen guys twitch with self-loathing after being unable to get a decent approach within 10 minutes of starting a night. In Pick Up, an Obsessive starts off a night with a one track mind, determined to succeed at all cost, but he ends up losing all his steam after 30 minutes in the field without tangible immediate outcomes.

When motivation is gone he starts looking for excuses, alibis, or simply gets mad. Obsessives tend to take women's rejection personally. They don't like making mistakes. But mistakes are the best way to learn in this game. So they quit after a while.

A Hacker likes the comfort zone. He learns one thing and he keeps repeating that one thing and doesn't want to learn anything else. Like a pitcher in baseball with only a fast-ball in his arsenal, he can't get himself to learn how to throw a curve ball.

Since he repeats his fast-ball all the time, the players in the opposing team learn and adjust their swings and start pounding it hard. But he refuses to learn to throw a good curve ball. Likewise, being a Hacker makes it impossible to progress in any game because Hackers refuse to learn anything new. Hackers don't want to take the baby steps required to learn a new thing.

A typical example of Hackers in Pick Up relates to those guys who learn how to start conversations with girls and do only that. They don't push interactions forward, they don't take the risk of being rejected, and they stick to what they know: chatting women up. They don't lead or escalate physically. Sooner rather than later, they find themselves frustrated because they don't get any girls.

One principle of the game (you need to lose girls, to get girls) reigns supreme. You must step up and do the uncomfortable thing, that is, escalate physically. Go for the kiss; pull her onto the dance floor.

A Hacker, unwilling to risk treading into unknown territory, impairs his own development.

Who Are You? Which Style Sounds More Like You?

Most people fall into any of the above-mentioned categories. I left out the mastery style on purpose, which I will explain later. However, you will find guys who are a mix of two categories. It's very typical so don't get worked up by it. In such a case, you only need to determine which way you tilt more. For example, if, on investigation, you find out you tend to get frustrated a lot, and you get super tense in the field, then you have determined Obsessive as your primary style with a bit of Dabbling mixed-in.

I also might add people go through all the learning styles as they get deeper into a practice. You might start off as an Obsessive, then become a Hacker for while and then end up Dabbling. I myself went through two of the learning styles when I learned to dance salsa. I first became an Obsessive. I wanted to become advanced in under three months— although it takes years. Then, when I found I couldn't be the best dancer on a salsa dance floor, I became a Hacker. I learned three moves and repeated them over and over.

I soon grew tired of my three moves. I was so bored with salsa that I wanted to quit. Then, in an unexpected turn of events, I discovered free styling in salsa. I learned the joy of improvising. I started to enjoy dancing again. Today, I am very conscious of my Obsessive qualities so I can manage my learning style and keep practicing and evolving.

You must know your learning style. If you are unaware, unknown forces will be unleashed upon you turning you into a helpless victim. You will quit before you have had a chance to learn.

Approval Seeking And Learning Style

One of my key discoveries when I started teaching this point to students was the direct relationship between approval seeking and learning styles. I don't care what anybody says, Pick Up revolves around approval seeking. Guys want to be liked at all cost. When that doesn't happen, they break down. As human beings we want a sympathetic audience.

However, looking for approval in a night club can mean death in this game. Why?

Because when girls like you, you will be motivated and on top of the wave, but when they don't, you will go under. Nobody can endure this rollercoaster all night, let alone four nights a week. Let's just say that in the field, you will not be stuck with picking up bitchy girls – but keeping your nose to the grindstone.

If you are a Dabbler, as soon as you don't get approval when you approach a group of girls, you will feel an urge to move on to the next. Your Dabbler always thinks the grass is greener on the other side. As a result, he will work group after group, but only remain for a very short time in each of them. He will end up talking to a bunch of girls but getting nothing. Positive regard will determine the depth of his dabbling pattern.

An Obsessive has different behaviour. If he doesn't get attraction – or strong signs of approval– in his first 20 minutes of approaching, he will get all frustrated and think he did something wrong. Motivation will go down and sooner rather than later he will quit.

On the other hand, a Hacker will stay within the realms of what he knows – namely, well-tested moves that will get positive reactions (another name for approval) every time. A Hacker will not push the envelope for fear of losing approval. For example, if he talks to a girl and gets good positive vibes he will not push for a make out or an extraction because he does not want to run the risk of being rejected.

In all three cases – Obsessive, Dabbler, and Hacker – approval seeking will determine how deeply your learning pattern runs into your game. In all cases, you must learn how to deal with your particular learning pattern. I will give you specific strategies to defeat the negative impact of learning styles. But before I do that I must introduce you to the master's learning curve. Pay attention because you want to get into this one right away.

How Masters Learn vs How Average Folks Think They Might Learn

First, I must show you how regular people think they will learn anything. If you are new to learning styles, you might think your progress would be linear. You start with no idea and in a progressive fashion you march onwards to become a master. Like this:

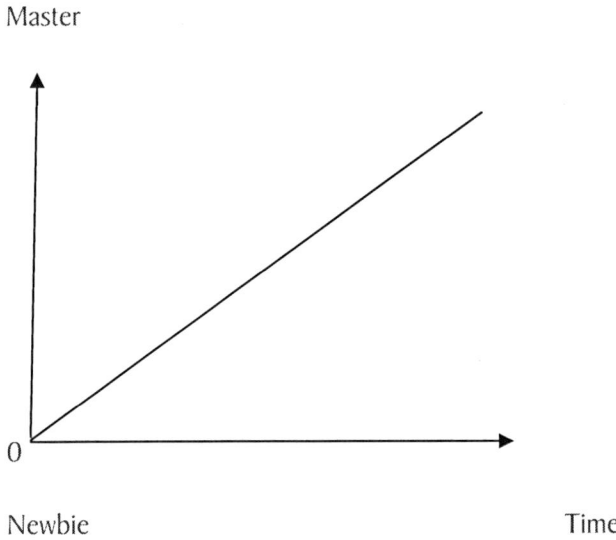

Nice, but untrue. Human beings don't learn this way because we are not robots. The above-curve illustrates unrealistic expectations about learning a skill.

The following diagram, conversely, brings us closer to the real world. Let me introduce you to the mastery curve according to George Leonard. This is, in a simplified manner, how people become masters at anything from playing badminton to driving a Formula 1 car.

Pay attention to the radical differences between the curve I have shown before and the following one.

The Physical Game

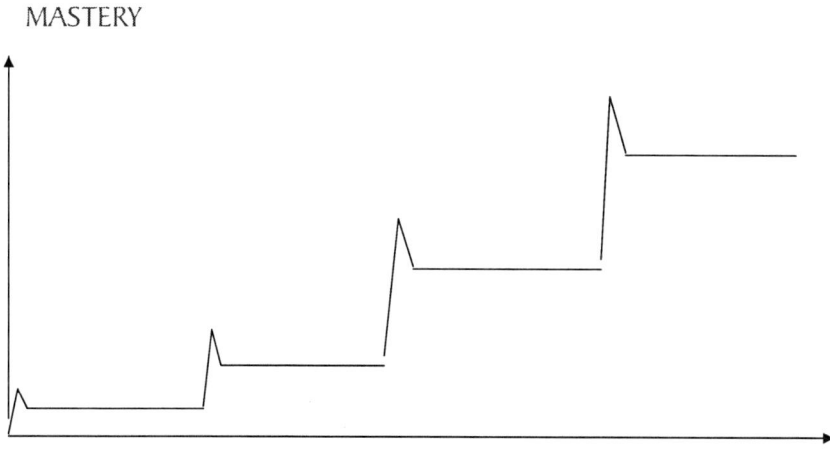

As you can see there are huge plateaus followed by peaks. The peaks represent climaxes, moments of gratification, which are followed by a slowing down into a plateau. Plateaus, ironically, are the meat of practice. Notice how this curve is radically unlike the layman's expectations of progress in learning.

To become a master, you need to spend long periods of time without huge climaxes – or cookies, as we call them in motivational science. Most people never become masters at anything because most people love the cookie. When they find themselves in long extended valleys of poor forward progress, they simply want another climax right then and there. Because no activity can meet such irrational expectations they quit.

Let's see how we can deal with this issue in Pick Up.

Zero Climax Dependence – Or Loving Your Plateaus

According to George Leonard people love the cookie. They want to feel good about themselves all the time – and for that reason they need climactic moments. However, in learning a discipline or a skill those moments are few and far between. We spend most of our time on a plateau. So we need to love them. Throughout the wear and tear of mundane practice, you need to be patient and realise that when you are on a plateau you are onto a good thing. You are where you are supposed to be. After all, valleys in our curve are but a sign of better times to come.

Let's say you have been approaching for 30 minutes in a club and, so far, you have got nothing– not even a 10-minute conversation with a girl. So you are on a plateau. You need to keep going and not look for a climatic experience in the first place. Your aim should not be getting approval to spike your self-worth, but getting into a talkative or functional state of mind. The game, unpredictable to the core, can delay your reward until the end of the night. So you must be patient and keep approaching.

You must think that if you get a girl 10 minutes before the club closes you are a winner in this game. You will forget about the three or four hours of zero climaxes you have been through. You will only remember the sweet moment when you struck an emotional connection and got your girl. You must remain positive whether you are getting your cookies or not. You can't get good otherwise.

Loving To Practice

Love of practice ranks at the top of a master's maxims. Most masters just enjoy showing up at the practice location. Just the feeling of being there excites them. Not necessarily because it means they are going to make tremendous progress that day but just because they like to show up and rumble.

I remember when I first went to a night club with no experience. I was terrified as I walked through the door. After some time, I was terrified to stay at home. I needed to go. The thrill I took from action became more powerful than my fear. To stay home was torture. I found my new comfort zone in the club.

You need to fall in love with the process of Pick Up, with your very practice of it. You need to crave walking into a club and meeting new people. Not only that, you want to enjoy talking to women just for the sake of it.

What would you rather be doing on a Friday night? Talking to a bunch of girls and having fun in a club or staying at home and watching TV?

Most guys realize they cannot stay at home anymore on a weekend after they have been in the field for a while. They miss the action. They'd rather be out there with girls and people rather than at home feeling miserable.

If you have a job where you work hard all week, then going to a club to meet chicks should be your reward. That was the way I used to look at Pick Up when I had an office job and was not a professional dating coach. I sometimes look back at those times and think of my trials and tribulations and feel good about it. I was excited to go out and learn. It was the most fun I ever had.

Be Prepared To Look Idiotic

Another illuminating tip coming from George Leonard himself: he claims masters are not afraid to look idiotic. They are not afraid to fail. They love to try new things and see how much they can get away with.

People who excel at what they do in any walk of life try the same things but in a different way. They are not afraid to experiment. They don't refrain from looking bad and becoming a child again, stumbling, falling and getting up. It takes honesty and mental flexibility to do that.

Often I have asked a student to approach a mixed group of guys and girls and the student has hesitated. I get the usual: "I have never done it before." When guys give me the "I have never done it before" excuse they mean: "I am afraid to do something I don't know the result of. What if I look stupid in front of those guys?"

If you feel that way, you must change. You must dare to look like an idiot sometimes in front of a bunch of strangers. Contrary to popular opinion being an idiot, making mistakes and getting it wrong are clear signs of somebody on the way to mastery of a skill.

Learn From Your Black Box

When a plane crashes, they look for the black box. I often wonder who gives a damn about how a crash happened. A bunch of people are dead. Nobody can bring them back. Of course, I am a lay man, which equals a moron in the avionics field. Because they study those accidents and learn everything that can go wrong, they have made every plane in the air today safer than ever.

Nobody wants to make mistakes. But when they do happen, we need to learn as much as we can from them. Not only that, but we even need others to look at them and give us their perspective. But people hide their mistakes. They want to appear perfect. So they hide their black boxes and, as a consequence, they miss major opportunities to learn and move faster to the next level. They end up turning small tiny errors into big, repetitive fat failures.

In Pick Up, if possible, I want you to write up everything you do during the night in the club. I know you might consider this gruelling and annoying. I know because I did it for years. However, when I wrote down what I did on a night, I had a second look at my actions. I could see not only my failures but also my successes. I recorded on computer files not only my good nights but my bad nights too. You can learn tons by having a fresh look the next day at what you did and get inspired to try it all over again.

Furthermore, I'd recommend finding a supportive internet forum (ie. www.rsdnation.com) and posting your write up there in a field report – and welcoming positive feedback. As your game progresses, more and more people will read your stuff, some with more experience than you are likely to pitch in, if they see you are honest about your endeavours. However, I recommend this as a secondary feedback. You should be able to learn from your own mistakes and your own opinion should always be the one you listen to first.

Ok, I think you have enough to work on for now. Just remember those tips as you apply the different techniques of physical game I am about to disclose. Let's move into how-to territory. The easy part.

Where To Stand When You Do Physical Game

I have already taught that you should initiate physical contact from the start and now I will teach you where you should stand when you start physical contact.

You must position yourself as close as you can to your girl. All Physical Game should be done from a close distance or it will look and feel awkward. As a top priority, you must cut the space between you and your girl. If you don't do this, you won't be close to her and therefore look creepy when you grab her. You need to get right in her face. Don't be afraid of body-to-body contact. That's what you are after.

Many people will have the following issue: "Isn't that invasion of personal space?" Yes. We are invading personal space. So what? It is not illegal or anything. A club is a no man's land where the rules that govern your office or society don't apply much. At a club level you must deem it both appropriate and necessary to take certain liberties like going for a make out five minutes after meeting a girl.

You must stand close to your girl from the moment you start talking. Get right into her personal space from the start. From there, your job of physical game becomes easier.

The Extended Handshake

Without much ado, you should introduce yourself and shake her hand and keep holding her hand for as long as you can. Once you get comfortable, you should be talking to girls and holding their hand without them being creeped out. It requires a lot of repetition. You might want to try it over and over and keep incrementing the time you hold her hand from seconds to minutes. It will look to others as if you are holding hands, but, in reality, you just extended a handshake into a holding hand pattern.

It helps if you smile as you do this and keep talking to her as you would in a normal conversation. Alternatively you can progress from a handshake to hold with ease. For example, pull your girl's hand you are shaking towards you and as she comes towards you, put your other arm around her shoulders in The Claw position. Now you are not only holding her hand, but you have your other arm around her shoulders. Talk to her from this position.

Hugs, High-Fives, Spinning

I put all these techniques together because they all are executed very much in the same manner.

Most people think they need permission to do any of these moves when in fact you don't. You need to start thinking in terms of giving yourself permission. For example, you ask a girl: "Where are you from," and she says: "Germany," and you go: "Fantastic, I love German girls. Give me five." And you proceed to high-five her. If you do this in a simple natural manner very few girls will resist. They will give you a high-five because you gave yourself permission to high-five her. Most Physical Game has to be done in this bold, confident, and straightforward manner for it to work.

The same applies to hugs, spinning, hip bumping and similar. You just take something she says and go: "That's fantastic," and initiate your move. Or: "You guys are from Germany, give me a hug!" and initiate your move. Though it's hard to resist a friendly hug, here and there you will still find a girl who won't comply. Don't fret over it. You need to fail to learn. Keep going. Other times, you will get a girl high fiving you with little or no enthusiasm; so, to patch it, you grab her hand and make her high-five with yours again. Say: "This is how you high-five," with a big smile on your face. It seems to turn them around. Yet, don't look for perfection in your practice, but consistency.

Same for the spinning move, you can say anything you want as long as you say it with smile on your face and in a fun mood. "Let me look at you!" and you grab her hand and motion for the spin. If you put her in a fun and friendly mood, she will graciously spin for you. If you don't, then you will get a lot of resistance. Keep practicing until you get girls spinning every time.

Hug And Hold, High-Five And Hold

I love to do this series of holding patterns. In fact, I keep trying them until I get my students to do them. When you hug and hold, after hugging, only half break your hug and stay with her with your arm around her shoulders. The same applies to high-fives: you high-five her and as she high-fives you back, you grab her hand or both hands (double five) and keep your hold for a while. You will look like you are both holding hands like a couple. Do this for as long as you feel comfortable yourself. Not her. Ignore her reactions as you do this. Though simple, it requires a lot of repetition.

Steady Physical Escalation

Most guys do the high-fives, the hugs, and the spinning and then they stop. They don't resume doing them. In their mind, they think they have done enough – yet they have done nothing. You are not supposed to do just a little bit of Physical Game.

The secret to get make outs is steady physical escalation. You keep spicing the interaction with all the above moves until the very end. You start slow, but you keep churning your butter until you get cream.

When I say: "Burn every interaction to the ground," I mean to take it as far as you can physically. How far are you willing to go? Your honest answer to this question will determine your level of consistency. Your willingness to lose girls will get you lots of girls. You want to push the envelope until either you get rejected or you make out with her.

Leading Her Physically: "Don't Ask, Just Take"

Here goes my first instruction on second night of my program when I plan to teach hardcore Physical Game: "Don't ask, just take." Never invite a girl to dance. Eliminate words like "Would you, Could you, Can you, Do you want to..." Instead, grab her hand firmly (I demonstrate the intensity of the grip by holding the student hand and asking him to hold mine back until he gets it right) and proceed to lead her to whatever you want to do with her. You can say "Let's..." and you can insert whatever you want there: "... dance to this song..." "... Go to the bar..." "... Move over here..." "...Sit down..." Then, firmly lead her through. In a nutshell, be dominant. Never ask for something you want, just take. Rude, no. Dominant, you bet.

Being dominant is about saying what you want, followed with action. After you tell her, you must grab her by the hand or wrist and pull her with you. It has to be done in a firm and dominant manner or it will not work. Once you do this many times and you get the hang of it, you will find women start to submit to you physically. Girls give in to a strong male presence. I don't care what the feminists say, the fact remains that most people, both men and women, will follow a strong leadership. Be it either social pressure to please a leading male figure or thanks to pure sexual attraction, leaders lead and others follow. Once you get in the habit of manhandling girls, the game becomes simple.

Where is your limit? I am very well aware I am teaching you to ignore when a girl says no. It sounds like harassment, but you have no choice. You must be blind to women's reactions to you. But there are limits.

In this we must exercise common sense. When I go in the club on my live programs, I say to guys: "Stop when a girl says she is going to call the bouncers on you or tells you to fuck off." That takes care of it. I never had any problems in five years of teaching that. We are all adults here and we know whether a rebuff is real or a test inviting you to further your interaction.

Token resistance is a given. Females would rather say "no" to a guy than "yes." They are programmed to do that. On the other hand, real objections to going with you feel different and you will be the judge. I trust you on that one.

Number One Short Cut to Leading Girls Physically

Here it goes: expect resistance.

For most guys, resistance is unexpected and catches them off guard. However, by expecting some form of front, you are in a better position. You are ready to plough through whatever they dish out.

When I pull a girl to the dance floor, I expect her to say "No." That's right. I know it is negative thinking but I am ready. In my head, I have a default behaviour: I will pull her, I won't take no for an answer.

Again, one of the principle questions of Physical Game: "Do you want to look good, or do you want to get laid?" must be adopted. I want you to look messy, but get it done. Like I have mentioned before, I want you to engage in a tug of war with her group for your girl. That's how bad I want you to look. You will build a thick skin to resistance that way. You do this enough, and you will become a master at pulling. Get it done, don't worry about what people think of you.

The Physical Game

Ploughing Through

You can use ploughing as another name for hardcore pushing through resistance. Like the historic Conquistador Hernan Cortez, I tell my troops (my clients): "Burn your ships." That's my way of saying never back off from a group. To be successful at approaching, you must commit to your groups 100 percent. You don't walk out on them, they must walk out on you.

Your limits are the same for escalation. If they tell you to fuck off, you better leave. Swallow your pride and walk away if they threaten to call security. No point in being red flagged in your favourite club.

Misinterpreting Bad Reactions

To defuse resistance, you just ignore their bad reactions or misinterpret them as being good ones. Women get a kick out of that because they see not only you have a sense of humour but that you don't buy into their bullshit either. You are just out having your own fun.

I instruct students to ignore negative remarks like: "Are you gay?" Or: "Where are your friends? Go back to them" Or: "You are annoying, go away".

Otherwise, I tell them to retort with something like: "You are the funniest girl ever. Give me a hug!" A friendly hug can defuse the tension and get people to forget their initial front and start talking to you. You must remain unreactive to women's dismissal and show them they don't affect you. Of course, this will take a period of trial and error before you educate yourself.

You must disregard a woman's emotions as a source of good feelings for you. Most guys feel good when girls give them positive reactions and miserable when women give them hell. But being your own source of good feelings goes a long way in becoming an attractive guy to the opposite sex. Self-amusement, being ready to look like a fool and not care, remaining unaffected emotionally by a girl's reactions are corner stones around which you build your game.

What's The Reward Principle?

If you want to become consistent at physical escalation, make it simple: reward good behaviour. If a girl smiles or laughs at something you said, grabs you, or show any sign of approval towards you, say: "You are the coolest, give me five" and high-five her. You can throw variety in by hugging her, spinning her, hip bumping her or whatever feels comfortable to you. You are just giving her a cookie for good behaviour.

Eventually, if you do this often enough, you won't have to initiate anymore. She will start high-fiving you, hugging you back without you telling her-they will give back whatever you give them first. You will see girls grabbing you, hugging you, leaning on you, pulling your arm without you asking them. It's the principle of rewarding good behaviour in action.

If you reinforce anything with a cookie, people will start giving it back to you. They start craving your approval. They start reciprocating your physical escalation. People mirror behaviour if it comes from somebody they want approval from. Like I have said before, this game revolves around female approbation.

Why Most Guys Can't Close The Deal

Either they wait too long or do it at the wrong time. You will find it all in the timing. Bear in mind when I say timing I don't mean waiting for, reading, or interpreting signals coming from a woman. I advise against becoming a signal reader because those guys don't take swift action: a guy meets a girl and he goes for the kiss after he has bored her to death. The same applies to your physical lead. Guys try to move their girl around or use any of the Physical Game techniques long after they have shown her that they are not fun at all.

Follow the golden rule: make your moves on highs. If you pull a girl on the dance floor when she is having a great time with you, you will have far greater chance than if you wait until your interaction winds down. Same thing when you are on the dance floor, and you are grinding cheek to cheek, and the sexual tension is high; this is when you make your move for the kiss. Rather than passively waiting for signals, you must capitalize on every opportunity to seal the deal. ABC – always be closing.

What's Running The Train?

After my two-hour talk in the DVD *Transformations* became wildly popular, many people kept asking me what "running the train" was. And I am compelled to answer: you can define running the train as going for the kiss, make out, extraction. That's to say, taking her out of the club to another location, physical escalation-getting physical with her. Anything resembling closing your deal. And going for it several times. It means running your train on a girl several times. No fear of failure, no ego protection, just behaving like a closing machine.

Behind running the train, you can find the principle of the game that every "no" is temporary. A "no" in this game means "not now", "not ready for it yet", "not sure". It never means "no", literally. You better believe it because if you don't you will be most inconsistent out there.

Most women will say "no" to your first attempt... and your second. I have a theory I have built over the years that a woman cannot say "no" more than three times. But that's just me. I could be wrong.

However, you must become a believer in this game. You must assume women want to say "yes" to you. You must become a hardcore, rock solid optimist. That's a challenge for most guys because your average male gives up at just a flick of a defiant eye from a girl.

Why Approach Seated Girls

I get the question, "But where do I sit?" every time. You have options: you sit next to her, but if you find no space, you either sit on her lap or you push her aside to make room for you. Guys don't like this answer very much. They want to be smooth and slide on to the seat next to her. But most times, there is no place to sit. Never kneel or squat when there is no room.

When I say to students: "Tell her to move and make room for you," it triggers a lot of resistance in guys. However, you establish your dominant frame by telling her to move away and make room for you. So it sets you off to a good start on the driving seat of attraction.

Remember to sit straight away unless you want to feel uncomfortable by talking down from a standing position. You must talk at eye level with each other. Don't stand there, leaning forward. She will perceive you have no authority and do not want to risk rejection by sitting down. All testing the waters for possible rejection must end if you are to establish yourself as a dominant male.

We want to approach seated girls because they last longer. Consider it a trap. Girls find it hard to stand up, excuse themselves and leave. On the other hand, you can get rapport faster by parking yourself down next to her. Physical game becomes speedier and easier when you are at such a close proximity. Seated girls account not only for the longest interactions, but also for a big chunk of make outs that my students get on program.

CHAPTER 7

The Infamous Ways Of Getting Physical Fast

Learn Timing For Physical Game With The Bully Approach. Watch How Girls Get Attracted With The Top Gun In Your Arsenal: The Legendary Technique Of "The Claw". And So Much More...

Why Fast? The Bully Approach

Most guys play safe when it comes to Physical Game (PG). They wait on the girl to give some kind of indication of interest or approval. Most Pick Up theories popular today share this principle in common: wait for an indication of interest before you initiate physical contact. I found teaching PG this way will stall 99 percent of the guys and throw them into passivity. Under the signals first rule, students of Pick Up talk forever and never seem to take action. I ended up frustrated with teaching the wait on cue method and switched to: "Assume she wants you and do it regardless." It seemed to work like a charm. Results soared. There was a huge increase in kiss closes and make outs, and guys seemed to get more confident faster and grew bolder as the live program unfolded.

Getting physical from the start of your interaction seems to teach the right things to both girls and guys doing it. Girls learn right away this guy means business and he relates to women in a physical manner. It teaches guys, on the other hand, that they can initiate interactions in a bold fashion without the fear of being rejected. In my experience, once guys learn Physical Game, they become such bulldogs that even rejection doesn't affect them as much. They become immune to it.

Strike First Theory

I was told growing up that if you strike first, then you strike twice. I am convinced of that in Pick Up. To attract a woman, you must take responsibility for your escalation right away – within minutes or seconds of starting the conversation. In other words, showing girls by taking control of the interaction that they only have to follow your lead. Thus, you take the responsibility off her and bring it onto yourself. Unwilling to be accountable for sex with a stranger, most women will appreciate it when you relieve her of that duty. So how fast should you start being physical? From the very start! Strike first, strike twice as hard.

Aside from taking responsibility for your interaction by being physical straight away, I would like to point out the elusive obvious: you will find it more legitimate to be physical than not. At club level you will find physical escalation happens fast or it doesn't happen at all. Either you are escalating or you are de-escalating. That means your interaction will become weird if you don't do something physical. Either you lead her through a series of small moves mentioned above (dancing, hugging, high fiving, or moving her around your club), or you will walk right into de-escalation.

A girl's interest will wane and die because you cannot keep momentum based only on conversation. Once you learn PG you will find talking kind of useless. You will rely on a physical rather than verbal lead. In countries where girls don't speak English, I resort to Physical Game on my live program. I am able to lead them despite the fact that I can't talk with them. PG has a language of its own.

If you don't believe this, think about what women say after a one night stand with a guy: "It kind of happened," or, "One thing led to another," or, "I was drunk." All of this indicates women won't take responsibility for going to bed with a guy they don't know. Knowing this inside information can be gold in the hands of a man who knows how to use it. It means we need to move fast on our target and keep leading her into making a series of small decisions (dancing, hugging, kissing, sitting down with us, taking her out of the club for food), until we make the last lead: taking them home with us.

Too Much *How-to?*

Excessive worry about doing it right will kill you in the field. You must be happy with successive approximation to your goal. Since you will never be perfect, do not think learning lots of tactics will make you a better player. It will hurt you because you will be busy thinking of what's best for a specific situation. This sorting out and analysing will get you stuck in a crowded venue.

Most people rely on gathering information. They think they will be better off with more information and make better decisions. Nothing is further from the truth when it comes to meeting women. Unlike stockbrokers trading on inside information, players in Pick Up need to keep moving forward through the night. Thriving on our need for prompt action, we don't want to fall into the trap of information overload. We want to roll in the field with one or two ideas at the most. No more. Instead of mindless pondering about the right course of action, I believe in simplicity and I enforce it to the max in a crowded, loud venue, where swift action is of the essence. You want to drop all the unnecessary baggage of extra information and travel with the bare essentials on a journey into a club.

Why Doing Something Poorly Works

My motto is "If it is worth it, get it done. No matter how." Do it poorly, but get it done. No place for perfection in this game. There are too many variables in play to worry about doing it with flawless panache. When you immerse yourself in practice, the last thing on your mind should be perfection. An excessive drive to faultlessness will kill an approaching practice based on experimentation. Even if I give you the right instructions, you will fail to make things work every time. So you must build a tolerance to failure and mistrials. Sometimes you will do everything right and get nothing. Other times, despite many errors and mishaps, you will end up with a girl back in your room.

If something is worth a try, try it. Don't wait. Better now than later. You should stop thinking about timing and execution. You should get into the habit of getting things done, even if poorly. In the back of your head you will say to yourself: "I did it, I didn't chicken out." You will grow confident even when you don't get what you want – because you tried. You didn't doubt yourself or back down.

Bold And Confident

After getting amazing results on their first night of my live infield program, novices get bolder. Last night's success fuels taking bigger risks their next day. Some of them trance out and become bold beyond control and overstep boundaries of social interactions and get away with it. Like a kid with a new toy, they play with female interactions. I went through something similar when I first started.

These days we teach a physical escalation technique called "The Claw." It's so effective at starting interactions guys love to play with it and get amazing results (make outs, girls all over them, girls offering numbers, etc.). They say: "This claw thing is freaking amazing, why didn't I use it before?" With these techniques they develop a new found confidence and they become super bold. But cheekiness doesn't get you laid.

For some guys, confident at their core, the effect of these changes lives on. However, for others, the ones that become only bold, the effect wears off and they slide back into old behaviours only days after. If they don't do the inner work required for being confident, they will not internalize the mindset of the game. Boldness doesn't yield confidence. However, confident people become bold.

Confidence means something different. You don't depend on Pick Up lines anymore – or girls' approval. You know who you are and you don't need a shield to hide behind. You Pick Up girls from your inner core, because you want to and you don't have to prove anything. Such cool demeanour will proclaim to women that they should either get with your program or get out of your sight. Because of you being nicer and more confident around others, people will like you – but not for the wrong reasons. People will feel drawn to you and want to chat because they sense you don't hide anything – a by-product of showing your true self in the open. You tell them who you are and let them judge you and welcome whatever reaction you get. Stripped of your approval seeking tendencies, you convey to them you are confident, not just bold.

Sexual Not Horny

You will find this hard to convey though. Let's put it this way: if you come across as horny, you will just freak out girls. Yet girls get attracted to confident sexuality.

Why doesn't horny work? It has been tried, believe me. By being horny you convey its ugly cousin, neediness. You are reaching. She feels you have little or no sexual choice. Your attempts to pick her up out of need not as opposed to natural attraction, will repulse her.

By picking her up out of need, not attraction to her, you proclaim to the world you could stick your penis in a hole in the wall and wouldn't know the difference. Coming across as desperate as your average 99 percent of guys in a nightclub looking to hook up is a bad plan. Your average club girl has become well aware of this needy behaviour. They will reject you on principle.

How Can You Be Sexual Without Being Horny?

I always resorted to being playfully physical. I remember this one guy we had in our crew who was in the habit of lifting a girl up like a sack of potatoes and putting her on his shoulder and walking away with her caveman style. You could hear her scream and shout as he carried her away.

Girls loved it. I am not saying you should carry women on your shoulder like he did (incidentally he was a big guy), but look at all the attractive qualities he conveyed when he did that: playfulness, boldness, confidence, manliness, not giving a damn, self amusement… The list goes on and on. He conveyed more by lifting a girl on his shoulder in one minute than you could communicate in two hours of storytelling.

PG can do wonders for you in this area when you try to convey sexuality without neediness. Leading a girl physically through grabbing her, pulling her by her wrist to the dance floor, spinning her around, will communicate those qualities aforementioned.

But You Still Want To Get Laid

Needless to say, I have been asked this question in every other conference where I speak. Do I go in with full sexual intent (aiming for sex) or fluff talk my way into deadly friend zone? You might find yourself misled by this apparent contradiction: sexual without being horny.

When I say sex should not be in your mind when approaching, I am trying to kill the horny, needy, sexually deprived weird man in you. You must eliminate those attraction killing vibes when you talk to women.

You must substitute them with a healthy, sexually playful vibe. You could talk about sex with a girl and say: "Sex? I don't do that anymore. I quit. I can't believe you like sex. I thought you were a homely girl. I am so disappointed," Sexually playful but not horny.

Alternatively, you can give her friendly hugs, high-fives, claw her whenever she does something you like – you layer on sexual components by being physical without being too needy. You keep reinforcing good behaviour every time with a physical cookie until you go for the make out. If you have done enough physical game in advance, making out shouldn't be a problem.

Looking Good Or Getting Laid?

I always ask guys on their second night of live infield program: "Do you want to look good or do you want to get laid?" Of course, they all want to get laid. But in reality as soon as they step into a club, they all want to impress. They want to execute without flaws. But that attitude will plunge you into a world of hurt – because tripping and falling means death for a perfectionist mind. You want to be as imperfect as you can be but you want to get your job done. I don't care if you engage in a tug of war with your whole group and a screaming chick that doesn't want to go with you – things can get ugly. Have the guts to not look good.

I don't want you to look for perfection in your execution, I just want you to grow some confidence in yourself out there and apply physicality into the game. Apart from pillaging and raping, I command you to go after what you want without making excuses. I want to see my students grabbing girls, dragging them onto the dance floor, and not caring how good they look as they do it.

The Physical Game

What's The Claw?

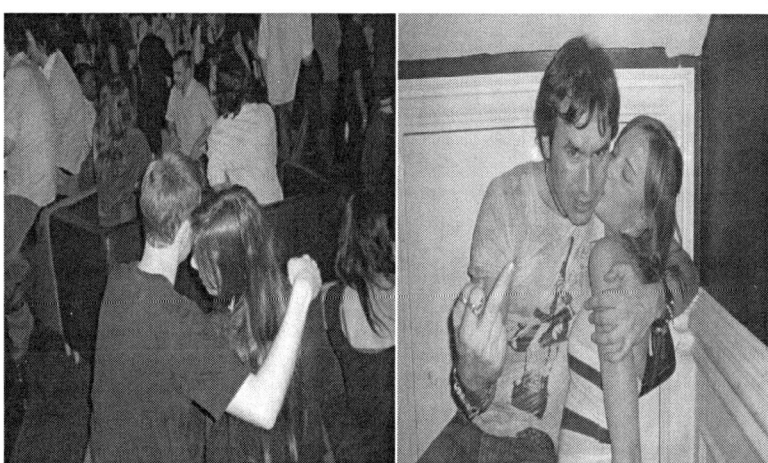

I kept answering this question in every workshop or RSD nation forum to the point I started giving funny answers like: "The Claw is the extended arm of god." Or: "The universe revolves around the mighty power of The Claw."

This truly amazing, simple tool does serve every purpose. It started as a joke between Tim (another RSD instructor) and I on a live program in Amsterdam. We started imitating guys who would creep out girls by putting their hand on their shoulder in an awkward fashion– and we both ended up teaching "The Claw" in our programs to great success. Many good things start in a joking way when you teach this discipline weekend-in, weekend-out.

The Claw couldn't be any more user-friendly: just put your arm around her shoulders as seen in the pictures above and hold your arm there for as long as you can. It's unsophisticated, but not easy. Most guys find this physical technique scary to execute. But believe me when I tell you that you will rip a lot of confidence and boldness out of this exercise. Practice your Claw at will until you get comfortable.

Why does it work?

The Claw, in one all-powerful stroke, communicates all the right things: dominance, authority, power. Comparable only to a nuclear weapon in warfare, this humble uncomplicated manoeuvre helps you apply all the principles of Physical Game at once. Using The Claw on an ongoing basis can lead to a high ratio of make outs and kiss closes. Most students who learn to use it swear by it. They love it so much they don't use anything else. "The Claw always wins," they chant in gratitude.

Timing For The Claw

The Claw can be thrown at different times during interactions. You can use it after a while of talking to a girl but, for best results, yank it out at the beginning. It might sound odd, but women love it. I know plenty of guys who open with The Claw. Sheer physical dominance in action. By using The Claw straight away you teach her the way you treat women or people in general. In general, by taking the risk first, you establish yourself in her mind as a super confident male who attracts women through his natural capabilities.

As a juicy side dish in your smorgasbord of seduction tools, The Claw will make women submit to you. They will yield to your strong hold on her shoulder. They will let their arms down in acquiescent position and go quiet as you run your game on her. Brought down by The Mighty Claw, girls, enter a trance of physical compliance to you.

Intended as an exercise to practice physical dominance, The Claw must be understood as neither a gadget nor a gimmick. As you throw your arm on a girl's shoulder, many will give you resistance. They will try to get away from under your arm. Keep her under your arm and hold your grip on her opposite shoulder for as long as you can. If you plough through resistance like this all the time you will grow empowered beyond compare. Women will submit to your advances more and more. However, as a pre requirement you must ignore reactions when you apply your Claw. You need to become un-reactive to your girl's emotions. Think of resistance and failed attempts as a sign of getting closer to your goal.

Train Hard, Pull Easy

Practice, practice and practice your Claw. You will learn lots from this great tool. Go by the small increment rule. Don't try to get it right every time. By trying to leave your Claw on your girl for longer and longer periods of time you will get good at being dominant. You will discover that girls start to take it after some time. Then you will start getting more make outs and bringing girls home.

Don't do it only to the girls you like. Do it to all the girls you meet! To get good at The Claw you must execute it every time you go out. There will come a time when you will do it with ease but in the mean time you must keep your nose to the grindstone. In all likelihood you will have to freak out a couple of girls here and there but so what: in the long run, The Claw will yield its results and you will have more girls than you can handle.

Part Four:
The Internals For Physical Game

CHAPTER 8

Belief System Transformation

If Your Belief Is Shaky, So Is Your Action. Assume The Gun Is Loaded: The Belief that Will Transform The Way You Interact With Women.

Shaky Belief Or No Belief?

Most guys start conversations with groups hoping the girls will not blow them out. With little or no belief in themselves, they get rejected on principle. This lack of belief has the disastrous consequence of making these guys appear weak or needy. You need to be different and think you are an awesome guy and that anyone would love to talk to you. This belief will make you consistent in the field. Thinking you have what it takes to open groups and engage women will help you get people's doors open in a crowded venue.

I tell my girlfriend: "Either you are pregnant or you are not. You cannot be half pregnant." That's belief in a nutshell. Either you believe or don't believe. Reality has a way of exposing somebody who doesn't have any real confidence in himself, but claims he does.

In this game, you cannot stand by the fence and watch the bulls. You have to jump in the ring and forget about the onlookers. To do this you need 100 percent belief you can make things happen for you. Anything lower than 100 percent will make you inconsistent. You will wither and die in the field as a consequence of lack of faith.

Allow me to explain why your beliefs are shaky now and what to do to correct this problem.

The "I Don't Deserve Hot Women" Belief

Haunted by horror stories of your past with women, you approach a girl only to communicate to her you don't deserve her. Your body language breaks; you mumble your words; you can't stand still. She sees through you. When you approach in this way, you will get nothing.

Though you might want to blame the girl for being dismissive, on a closer look at your approach, you will notice it had to do with you and your shaky belief system.

The painful obviousness of truth: if you don't believe you can get her, you won't. It's the way of all things. Chances are you haven't buried your unsuccessful past with women and you are still living there. It will take you some time before you start changing the way you think of yourself in relation to women. I will try and make this process faster for you. In your replacing of old convictions with new ones in regards to women you must put an emphasis on shining.

Some Obvious Things We Need To Get Rid Of First

There are certain common male thought patterns that communicate themselves to a girl. The "I don't deserve you," patterns. We need to weed them out first in order to gain some clarity.

First of all, you must stop all hovering, leering, lurking and standing around your girl and delaying the approach. Nothing alerts a girl to "I don't deserve you" more than you standing like a guard around her and trying to muster your courage to talk to her. By doing this, you not only jump in the pool of horny men around the club– she thinks you are one of them – but also, in the process, you spook your girl out. She will feel you are stalking her.

Other unwanted behaviours are very obvious. Think: types of supplications like buying her drinks, complimenting her on her eyes, asking where she got that dress. All these things communicate that you are not in her league. It tells her you are going way out on a limb by talking to her and you need to resort to bribery and cheesy compliments to get anything going. Those repellent ways of relating to females must be eliminated on principle.

To Get Girls You Have To Lose Girls

The following example happens all the time on my program. A guy approaches all night without a single rejection. Women seem to love him as they laugh at his jokes... For an onlooker it might seem as though he never gets rejected and therefore excels at chatting women up.

But nothing could be further from the truth. First of all, those guys come to me because they can't get girls. Some have been years without getting laid. Why? Though they seem socially savvy they don't risk anything in their interactions. They play safe all night and, though surrounded with female approval, go home alone. I always say there are two types of guys who never get rejected: those who never approach and those who don't take risks. If you are not getting rejected enough, you are not going to get laid enough. In order to get girls, you must lose girls. Simple.

Becoming Invisible To Women vs Asserting Your Reality

Because of the basic assumption that the more they like me, the better I am, you sacrifice your authenticity. You become an act, not a real person. Instead of conveying your true personality you choose to entertain them. In this process, you sacrifice your real self. In other words, women don't get to see or interact with the real you. You become invisible.

Her reality takes over yours as a consequence of this act. Because you don't assert your reality, hers gets affirmed. You hear women say to you: "What do you want from me?" Or they imply it by saying: "Where are your friends?", hinting you should go back and entertain them and leave her alone. You are wasting their time.

Other times, with more subtlety, your conversation revolves around what she chooses to talk about. Her reality keeps getting asserted while yours gets shut down. At this point, guys find the conversation going nowhere, which in Pick Up language means that you failed to assert your reality. You ran out of entertainment and she took over. You became invisible.

Changing Core Beliefs To Change Behaviours

Once you boil it down, you find beliefs at the bottom of how we conduct ourselves. We act according to those beliefs. The behaviours

I described before are just a by-product of certain beliefs we acquire over time. They shape who we are today and how we act.

For example, some people tend to think, "money doesn't grow on trees," and so they go on in life being poor and scraping a living. It isn't the bad economy but their faulty belief that there is not enough money that keeps them from wealth. Even with a booming economy, most people will remain poor because of what's known today as scarcity mentality. You cannot get something you don't believe to be in abundant supply.

Same happens with women.

If you have a certain belief around women like "hot women are rare", then you won't find them. Everything you do will be tainted by this faulty belief. You will have a hard time running into hot girls because beliefs tend to reinforce themselves. In other words, you will be looking for supporting evidence for this conviction of yours. You will walk around malls, tube stations, and streets only to find there are a lot of ugly women out there. Being outside your area of awareness you will not think of looking up the top clubs in your area where the hottest girls in town gather. Your assumption prevents you from awareness.

Install New Beliefs

Let's run through the following exercise. Read the following sentences and think which of the two sounds more like you. Be honest.

"People are always friendly"

"People are out to get me"

Those two sentences represent two different and opposing beliefs.

Most people favour the second. Interestingly, some assumptions were implanted in your brain a long time ago. Mothers are responsible for brainwashing their kids with ideas like don't talk to strangers, so kids grow up thinking interacting with other people can hurt them. But guess what: the belief that helped you survive childhood no longer applies in an adult, interdependent society. In fact, it can be counterproductive when approaching women. If you swear by the idea that it is not safe to talk to strangers, when you approach a group of people in the club, you will be fearful, uncomfortable and you will spook them away. Or, worst of all, you will not dare to approach.

Let's get deeper into how beliefs shape your behaviour. Say, for example, you have the all too common belief that people are out to get me. What do you think your body language will be like when you step into a club?

For starters, you will display defensiveness (like crossing your arms, occupying as little space as possible). You will also probably find a corner where you are not noticed. Furthermore, you won't approach anybody because of your fear of the repercussions. Will you get any girls that night?

Now, let's for a moment think you are a delusional (beliefs are delusional by nature) positive cool dude who thinks that people are always friendly. Then, you walk into a club thinking positively and thinking that people are always friendly. What do you think your body language will be like?

I am sure you will have what I call an "expansive" body language: open arms, chin up, smile on your face, comfortable, occupying a lot of space. You could stand in the middle of the crowd and engage the first group you see in an amicable conversation.

Now, for your million dollar question: which of your two guys will have a better chance of taking a girl home that night? By long and far the guy thinking that people are always friendly. Become that guy by acquiring the belief that will have the greatest impact on your reality.

You might think that thinking people are always friendly is unrealistic and you might be tempted to change it to: "people are sometimes friendly," for the sake of truth. But it doesn't work that way. Beliefs need to have this delusional quality to them to work. Your beliefs need to push you out of your comfort zone and challenge your set of ordinary assumptions. In other words, a belief must have an unbelievable component to it for you to get on the right track.

Can't Dream It, Can't Do It

I have always had trouble making a student do something he cannot imagine himself doing. While in a state of altered reality, you must visualize yourself already in possession or enjoying things you don't

Ozzie

have. Like the courage to approach women, getting physical with them, getting them to have fun with you, etc. Visualizing has proven useful in NLP as well as in every other success-teaching system in the market today. Why not use it for Pick Up too? Visualisation and belief system transformation has been and continues to be used these days because, unlike a fad, it works.

We need to acquire beliefs that serve our purpose of meeting girls. Conversely, we need to discard those that won't help us or might become a serious obstacle to our goal of meeting as many women as possible. Let's explore those beliefs that are going to be useful to us, shall we?

How Assuming The Gun Is Always Loaded Will Help You

Welcome to the first rule of gun handling: Assume the gun is always loaded. This type of assumption or belief helps people be safe when they deal with guns. I find it particularly helpful in Pick Up. I fell in love with it because it changes your paradigm. If you ever deal with guns you will know what I mean.

When I was a child, one of my uncles had an old 16-guage shot gun. My uncle would load it with empty shells for me so I could play with it. Sometimes we went shooting for real and the gun was loaded all the time. Believe me, you are very careful when you handle a loaded gun. Safety becomes a priority – no more playing. To be on the safe side when picking up lots of girls, you need to assume they are all loaded (attracted) when you handle them. You need to think you can shoot for real every time.

To be successful you must assume they all want you. Looking at women like they are all into you will have a profound effect on your results. First off, you will be confident around them because they want you; second, you will avoid attraction killers like trying to impress them (because they want you already) or trying to be too nice or too friendly. Moreover, by having this mentality, being physical with them will become simpler. Remember if you don't get physical, your interaction doesn't move onto the sexual lane.

Most guys, because of low self-esteem in this area of their lives, have a faulty belief: "I am not lovable as I am." In the back of their heads, they think they need to do something to a girl or get permission from her to initiate any kind of physical contact. However, most successful guys with women think they are incredibly attractive and most women will be lucky just to be with them. They harbour beliefs like: "All women want me," or, "I am attractive to all women."

Notice how delusional these beliefs are – but also notice how effective they can be to with females. By assuming the gun is always loaded (read: "all women are attracted to me") these men are able to behave in a manner around women that subliminally communicates to girls they are deserving of them, rather than conveying an "I am not lovable" vibe.

If you have a delusional belief like, "all women want me," you will be more comfortable around them, and you will have zero problems– not only initiating physical contact straight away, but also maintaining it throughout your interaction.

Permission To Be Physical. Or, Signal Reading, A.k.a. I.O.I Junkie

When I first started practicing Pick Up, it was viewed as a huge miscalibration (another jargon word for doing something stupid at the wrong time) to initiate unwarranted physical contact with a girl. Five years ago everything was about controlling your interaction to the last detail. Controlling implied you had to make the right moves at the right time in a linear sequence of Open-Attract-Rapport-Close. Such a linear approach was beyond questioning. Most practitioners in the field accepted it on faith.

What this meant in an interaction was that we had to wait for three approval signals (or I.O.I's) minimum from a girl, to indicate she was ready to move to the next level. Some of those I.O.I's (a.k.a. indicators of interest) were girl touches her hair, girl bites her lips, girl touches you first, girl laughs at your jokes, and so on. We were not only reading the girl's body language all the time for I.O.I's but also, more importantly, we became obsessed with producing those very signals or signs of approbation.

Thus, we became I.O.I. or approval junkies.

In other words, if we didn't get those signals of approval it meant we were not doing a good job. So every night we went out to hunt for positive regard from women. Fortunately you don't find that kind of mentality any longer these days.

Basically, in the I.O.I. based system we were looking for permission to escalate from outside. Unless your girl gives you green light you will refrain from physical contact.

But, on the contrary, in our gun-is-always-loaded system, we give ourselves permission. We self validate. We assume she fancies us right off the bat and we go for it from the beginning. We don't try to get her approval because we think we've already got it.

Get Physical Without Permission

That's a hard one. What needs to happen for this mentality to work? You need to believe that *everything is an I.O.I.*

That means you interpret everything a girl says or does as meaning that she wants you. And I mean everything. Bad reactions are included too. And however delusional, believe me, you have no other way but delusional to go about this.

Let's say she says: "Go away, I hate you." You need to train yourself to believe she means to say: "I want you." But for how long and how much rejection can you take before you walk away? Where is your limit? I say when she threatens to call the bouncers on you. We back off because we don't want to get into trouble over one girl, when there are hundreds prancing around in a venue. But anything other than threatening to call security you must consider fair game.

This type of mentality of not walking away will not only help you to grow a thick skin to rejection but it will also strengthen your breaking resistance skills. Ploughing through a girl's front encompasses a huge part of Pick Up. Most girls are programmed to give you some form of resistance throughout an interaction. You won't find it a smooth sailing every time if you are serious about getting laid. You can count on struggle. If you approach a lot of women, resistance will be there more often than not.

But as you practice your Physical Game techniques and get more confident, you will see resistance going down as your skills go up. A by-product of repetition and practice the more you withstand opposition, the better you get at bypassing it. Then as you get confident, you will see girls opening up to you faster and faster no matter what you do. Rebuff will become an opportunity for you to show her the persistent man you have become. Trouble breeds opportunity. However, I must warn you: you need a strong set of beliefs to make this work. Let's explore this part in more detail...

How To Get Yourself Believing That You Are the Programmer, Not The Program

"A belief happens after a lot of evidence is piled up."

Not really. Some girl you fancied rejected you in high school and you, all of a sudden, started believing: "Girls don't like me for who I am." Or: "I am not likable." One single girl not liking you cannot be considered an awful lot of evidence, but still it shattered your confidence. It helped create a new self-limiting conviction about the opposite sex.

The reason was you liked this particular girl and you witnessed her rejection to you. You saw it all unfolding in front of your eyes. That's how beliefs are formed. You need to see it to believe it, no matter if it was one time only. Your mind got busy from that moment on finding new evidence that you were right to think: "Girls don't like me for me." And proof you found, to the point you stopped trying. That's what a negative belief will do to you. It will send you rocketing into paralysis.

Unfortunately, most feel they are the program – the belief system. Those negative assumptions become an intrinsic part of their identity and they cannot change them. However, you are the programmer, not the program. Those faulty convictions are the software, not you.

If you don't like your present program running your head, you can change it.

You are your system administrator. You can change your operating system as many times as you like. However, you have never attempted to change it or have grown to feel helpless in this area. Because belief systems are like tracking programs, once installed they will get busy trying to track evidence to support themselves and survive. In other words, your program will try to justify its worth. It sounds like *Matrix* movie stuff but it doesn't get any more factual than this.

How does this programming apply to picking up women? In this game, you need to believe it to see it. You need to believe they want you already for them to be attracted to you. The more you think it, the more evidence you will find to support your belief. In other words, your mind will get busy finding evidence to legitimise your faith.

For beliefs to work, they require an incubation period. The length varies with the person. I have installed a new belief in a student after half an hour of approaching in a club. The student rolled in with no evidence women liked him, but only a few good interactions with females here and there, helped reinforce the belief that: "I am an attractive man."

I like to think it was not a miracle. His mind, imbued with a new belief, a new tracking program, was looking for validating evidence and found it. Some minds don't need much proof. Others never admit the evidence. I know plenty of guys in the game who after having tremendous success with women still believe they are defective items. They still think girls don't like them for who they are. Just like a depressed geek on the internet sporting a super fun avatar fools people, those guys have built a Pick Up persona to attract women— not real, a construct. Sad, but true.

Now, if you commit to your beliefs, I guarantee you will soon experience a shift in behaviours. Let me explain this part more in detail.

Building From The Ground Up

Different beliefs will cause different behaviours to appear – from body language changes to the way you interact with people. A different behaviour creates a different reality. And a new reality must be your ultimate goal.

Read your formula for reality change:

New beliefs+ New behaviours = New reality

Most people try to implement or copy new behaviours, but fail to create new realities. Then your behaviour is fake, for it has no solid ground under it. It happens when students try to mimic an instructor's behaviour, but find themselves getting negative results. A behaviour, unlike a belief, you can define as an action you take – something you do. However, when you believe something, you don't have to fake or do anything to prove it. It is self evident because you live by it. A strong conviction will create a strong and consistent behaviour. And a new reality will follow in kind.

> *Reality Check*
>
> *An example of this contradiction between behaviour and belief happens when I instruct a student to walk up to a girl and get physical from the start. This new behaviour finds opposition thanks to his belief: "Girls don't like me for who I am." His new behaviour that sees him: "Getting physical from the start and assuming she likes you already," finds opposition in: "Girls don't like me." So a conflict appears, which leads to paralysis. Your average student might do something only when I tell him to do it. But left unsupervised, he would do it on and off, and inconsistency would rear its ugly head. This conflict happens when beliefs and behaviours are not in alignment. It results in a conflictive inconsistent reality being created.*

People who make things happen believe they can. In a nutshell, to create a new and radical reality (lots of women, threesomes, sex life of a rock star) you need new and radical beliefs. In order to sustain a new reality, beliefs must be reinforced and repeated on an ongoing basis. So far I have not said anything most motivational theories haven't said before.

Let's apply it to Pick Up.

Become Gimmick Free

Drop all gimmicks and go for the real thing. Find new beliefs in alignment with the kind of reality you want to have – and get in the process of implementing them through new behaviours. In other words, if you run your mind under a faulty program, realize you are your programmer and change your program anytime you want, however you want. Also understand you're not hopeless and check if victim-thinking or self-defeatism has a hold on you at this point. Don't look for shortcuts or quick fixes because there are none.

New beliefs need to be repeated all the time to hold. Thus, you must reinforce your new program or you are likely to keep using your old one. Let's see how we can do this.

Your Road to Being Effortless

Affirmations are a good way to go about this. I suggest writing down your affirmations MANY TIMES. When you pencil something down, it gets burned or tattooed in your subconscious. I recommend penning affirmations down in the morning when you get up and before bedtime. Write you positive conviction down on a piece of paper 20 or 30 times. Do this for a month and check if your behaviour has changed. Repeat as needed.

Alternatively, to make sure you don't forget, stick your beliefs on the wall above your toilet seat or on your mirror so you can re-read them every morning, before bedtime and when you go to pee.

Furthermore, you can repeat your affirmations when you are in practice mode in the club. For example, as you walk up to a girl, repeat to yourself: "It is fun to approach." If you do this long enough, approaching people becomes fun. It turns effortless because you are having fun doing it.

I also instruct that it is ok to make mistakes. Students repeat this as they approach a new group of people. By saying this to themselves, they help their performance anxiety drop to zero and they are able to do a better job. Things become effortless because mistakes stop being a threat.

Other affirmations (such as: "Everyone is always friendly") can help you further change your beliefs about other people. The more you repeat this in your head, the more people get friendly to you. Your new belief finds evidence in the real world to support itself. The more proof you find of friendly people, the stronger the conviction grows, in a snow ball effect. Over time your behaviour will change around people and reality will follow in kind. You will make more friends faster.

Affirmations For Obsessive Types

"I am enough," "I am ok as I am" are among other positive affirmative phrases I use with students with Obsessive behaviours. Obsessive guys look for things to fix. "Seek and you shall find" – or so goes the saying. If you scout for things to mend in your personality, you will find them big time and make them bigger. Repairing defects sounds good on first analysis, but proves devastating when you are trying to master the art of talking to people.

If you look for things to repair, you will forever be reacting to problems and trying to find solutions. For an Obsessive, it feels like playing a "whack a mole" game. This game is an attraction in fairs where you are supposed to hit a mole's head with a hammer as soon as it comes out of a hole. However, with lots of holes to cover, as soon as you hit one mole's head, two others pop up.

That's how it feels to be an Obsessive trying to fix parts of your personality. Not the problem itself, but the way you see the problem *is* the problem. You look at yourself as a defective item in need of repair. Every time you get rejected, you feel incomplete. Therefore, you get obsessed with fixing the problem. But rejection is part of the game. People who don't get rejected don't get laid. You cannot eliminate the rejection problem because it comes with the job of bedding lots of women.

I would like to finish with a drill I use to cure Obsessive patterns. It can be used also as a warm up drill at the beginning of your night in case you walk in the club and do not feel like approaching girls.

> ### COACH DRILL
> **Befriending the Room.**
>
> Make friends for 30 minutes with the whole room. Do it as you arrive in a venue – when you don't know who is who yet. Despite the fact you might feel you are doing something lame when you talk to girls without an end in mind, keep doing it. Don't let bad reactions change your belief that people are always friendly. Instead, focus on those who are friendly to you and make it evidence of your new belief. You might be pleasantly surprised when you are talking to some dude and he happens to be the leader of a big group and he introduces you to everybody in it, including the single girls. By winning his seal of approval, you get your free pass to the group. Working the room for friends opens unexpected doors for you and reinforces a key conviction in the game: "People are always friendly."

CHAPTER 9

Perception Is Reality

*Discover Why Some Approaches Don't Work
And How To Correct Scarcity Mentality*

The Way We See the Problem Is the Problem

If I were to summarise this chapter into a phrase I would quote Einstein's: "You cannot solve a problem with the same mind that created it." I found this to be true when it comes to getting girls and having the sex life of your dreams. For example, if you place too much importance to getting laid, chances are you will not get laid. You cannot solve the getting-laid problem with a scarcity mentality and thinking that beautiful girls are scarce and hard to get.

In other words, if you have a faulty map you will never get to where you are going, no matter how hard you try. You will end up in the wrong place. People with faulty head maps find themselves reaching unwanted destinations all the time. They must realize that their map and the territory they are treading on differ.

Let's walk you through the world of perception in Pick Up and how to dial perception right so we can approach the problem with a different mind.

What is Putting Girls On A Pedestal?

Most guys who don't get laid tend to think girls are hard to get. They develop a scarcity mentality around girls, which turns into a problem. When they are scarce you say to yourself: "Girls are a highly sought-after item." Or: "There are not plenty of them for everybody." Or: "I must get their approval or I will lose my one chance to get laid with a beautiful girl." You will increasingly perceive women to be in control of the situation. It's very disempowering, to say the least, when you dial your perception this way.

I have noticed guys who have tremendous success with women don't attach much importance to getting laid anymore. They already have a steady supply of women so they are not stressed about it, which in turn makes them more attractive to the opposite sex. They are not afraid to lose girls or take risks because they know deep down they don't need them so much. They have an abundance mentality around women: they think there are plenty of women to go around. As a consequence, women don't feel they are being put on a pedestal or granted a free pass because they are beautiful. And this creates massive attraction because females get a sense you are in control.

Perceived Value vs. Real Value

When you have the scarcity mentality mentioned above women's value to you skyrockets. You think you don't have what it takes to get females. Thus, women become and object to get (a "target" in Pick Up jargon) another extension of the effect called objectification of women. Attractive females, devoid of their human quality, become an object to get, collect and use. You stop looking at them as people with feelings, needs and wants.

As a punishment for such a moronic way of looking at the opposite sex, women's value will become much higher than yours. You are going to find yourself out of control when you interact with them. Imagine yourself outside a vintage car dealer in awe of a beautiful car, peeking and pressing your nose against the glass window. They, women, will be in control.

To illustrate my point, I am going to give you the Ferrari analogy. When you objectify women you will perceive no difference between a Ferrari and a hot girl. The same thought –I wish I could have it, but can't – will cross your mind when you see a beautiful girl walking by.

But while this might be true for the Italian car (you might not have the funds at hand), it can never be true for a girl. You can have her. You don't need hundreds of thousands of dollars to approach her. And I tell you more; you can have her and dump her later for a hotter one. It only takes looking at her with a different mind and taking a genuine interest in her as a human being, not as a valuable collectible item.

> ### Reality Check
>
> *If you look at a girl as a collector's item- a scarce object- you run the risk of feeling you don't deserve her. These feelings will be translated into all kinds of vibe killers and/or approval seeking behaviours on the approach. You will be perceived as needy and inferior.*

How It Works

"Look over your shoulder, the girl is super hot," I said to one of my students on one of my live programs. "You didn't realize how hot she was when you interacted with her because you were in zero approval state."

> ### Reality Check
>
> *When you are looking for approval, not only do you look at people as objects but you also avoid approaching those you feel have a higher value than you. You feel you are not worthy of talking to somebody better than you. When you are not looking for approval but self-amusing in the club strangers become friends.*

Looking at people as humans, not as targets, will help you feel at ease and will erase the common value judgments you make as you step in a club. Nobody will feel higher or lower than you. You will behave as if you are just talking to people, not seeking consent from them. You will have what I call a clean vibe stripped of supplication or approval yearning. People will feel you are not there to take value from them rather to contribute. You will not be affected by superficiality like physical looks or external signs of status like dress, jewellery, or similar.

How People Fake It In Clubs

I must be honest with you: superficiality runs wild in clubs. You can't find real people. People have shallow interactions: they dress to impress, they show off their wealth by renting bar booths or buying expensive drinks to get attention, and so on. You must aim not to be affected by all this shallow front. You need to get to a zero approval seeking point every night. In doing this most of those very people, because you are not aiming for attention from them, will start craving approval from you. To achieve this you must not be shaken by an adorned exterior and treat everybody as an equal. You must not be misled by first impressions.

In order to illustrate my point I must relate The Fatman Story, a story about first impressions and how misleading they can be.

Some time ago I was running a live program in London during the heyday of the investment banking industry in the city, prior to the credit crunch. Venues were inundated with financial high rollers splashing cash left and right, buying expensive champagne and throwing I-am-the-richest-guy-here parties and generally showing off their newly acquired wealth and status.

In this context, I was running my program. All of a sudden, I saw a fat guy in a tux with a bottle of champagne in his hand walking in, flanked by two model-type girls, one blonde, one brunette. He looked like your typical successful investment banking manager having a night on the town.

We approached them and my students got a hold of the two girls while I chatted to the guy. To cut a long story short, the students separated the girls from the guy and very soon the truth came out. This guy had met these girls that afternoon, paid for the limo drive to the club, the champagne and both girls' dinner. He was a chump. The girls confessed they were using him to get in the club and pay for their night out while they looked for real dates.

Needless to say, I saw him walking around alone later that night still holding on to his French champagne. He had lost his girls after paying dearly for them. However, we didn't know this information coming in. The guy was faking because he knew coming into the club with two hotties would make him look good. At first, we just saw a dress-to-impress guy flanked by two stunning girls. Because we didn't assume he was higher value or better than us we approached them on principle. We didn't let our superficial judgement kick in.

Most guys let those superficial values take over their ability to approach. Notice how we didn't say: "I wish I could be that guy," or assume: "Those girls must be his sexual slaves." Most of all, we didn't look at the Ferrari from the window, our nose against the glass; instead, we considered them equals and approached them in kind. Never believe what you see and don't assume anything in a club – for it will never be the entire truth. Seek to learn, be curious, and investigate.

The Pull Of Superficial Values

Don't let superficial values drag you under. I cannot stress enough the value of being unassuming and non-judgemental.

You don't know who is who.

Be humble, seek to learn, investigate and talk to them. I follow the maxim that everybody is innocent until proven guilty. I won't allow myself to think otherwise. However, most guys think, "Everybody is guilty." For example, if they see a guy with a girl they jump to conclusions and assume him to be her boyfriend. Yet on further investigation, you realize 90 percent of the time a random guy with a girl is a friend, roommate, or an orbiter (a guy who follows her around but won't close the deal) or a random dude, just like you, she met in the club.

Assumptions, assumptions, assumptions. But your gold-medal worst assumption ever reads: "She won't be into me."

Guys make that assumption with girls they consider out of their league (read: the type of girl they never had). You can substitute: "She won't be into me," for: "She is better than me," or: "Too good for me." It sounds like your average Ferrari syndrome. "I don't deserve a car like that." "I wish I had the funds to buy one, but I don't."

To change you need to make a complete leap of faith. You must commit to the mantra: "Meet the person behind the pretty face." If you see a pretty girl, be unaffected by her beauty and meet the person. If you focus on her good looks, you will start seeking approval from her. Conversely, if you look to meet the human being behind the pretty face, you will be curious about her and you will search, investigate, and find out whether you would like to spend time with her.

When you meet the people, not their painted exterior, you won't be looking for approval. People will be emptied of their external value. As a consequence, their consent won't have any pull on you. You won't be needy. When my students reach zero approval point or 100 percent expression point, as I call it, they don't look so much at the externals of people but focus on other things like fun, being themselves, playing around, busting on the girls.

Because your mind cannot focus on two things at a time, when you focus on the person, you won't pay attention to external symbols of value. You won't notice them as much. Approaching becomes simpler.

What's Your Agenda When Approaching?

Most guys approach thinking: "Let's see if I can attract her." Or: "Let's see if she likes me." However, this only serves to make them walk up and start looking for approval right off the bat. As a by-product of trying to create attraction rather than assuming attraction they turn into entertainers/Pick Up robots.

I am all for the latter: assuming attraction. For in the former you are at the mercy of things you cannot control. Your attracting her depends ultimately on her. Like stepping in a mine field, you won't know when you are going to blow up.

On the other hand, if you assume she wants you, you will only try to find out if you like her back. In other words, as your working agenda, you must investigate if you are attracted. That will put you right in the driver's seat. You will talk to her to see if she happens to be somebody you want around all the time, not just in a club.

Hidden Turn Offs

Guys fall in love with a girl just by looking at her in the corner in a club. They go: "She is hot, I wish I had her." Her value goes through the roof in the guy's eye.

Let's say you are 100 percent attracted to her because of her beautiful looks. You are ready to go and meet her. Let's suppose, for the sake of proving a point, that I know everything about her because we grew up together. And then as you get ready to approach, I whisper in your ear: "she has two kids" – a deal breaker for many guys. Now, look at her again.

Do you notice how your perception changes? Maybe you went from 100 percent attraction to 80 percent. She dropped 20 points on the spot. Now I tell you further: "She has had her left breast removed."

Now, look at her again.

Do you still consider her desirable under the light of this new information? So you went from 100 percent attraction to 20 or maybe zero. Do you still want to meet her? What if I told you she was pregnant or she was a hooker trying to score clients? Just kidding.

In a night club, what you see is not what you get. Appearances deceive. You won't know until you meet her. That's why you should assume nothing, drop all value judgements and shouldn't be disoriented by superficiality.

Value Or Hotness Is Relative To The Girl, Venue, Situation, Country

The more I dig into the concept of a girl's value through direct experience in various clubs, different countries and venues, the more I get more inclined to stop talking about it. A girl's value can be so relative and subjective; it doesn't stand any serious scrutiny. As a theory, it has so many holes you might as well forget all about it.

For example, a girl's perceived hotness in a venue is relative to the other girls in the same venue. If she has better looks than any girl in that venue, she will stand out from the crowd with no effort and, thus, she will start acting stuck up. She will behave like a precious commodity.

However, the very same girl may be just average looking for a high scale venue full of model types (I am thinking of some exclusive LA venues), where she might be more open to talk to guys because her perceived value has dropped. Furthermore, if she feels overpowered by the fact that there are so many attractive girls around, she might go hormonal, make up an excuse and go home. Her value is shattered by superior competition.

There are countries with an unusual supply of hot women like Sweden. It's not a novelty to be good looking there for a woman, but an average Swedish club girl will stand out in any other part of the world. So when you are in Sweden, you don't feel so much the pull of value judgments or so many "she is out of my league" thoughts. You do not have a frame of reference to compare value because the supply of hot women is abundant and they all look the same. And because of your abundance situation you won't be afraid to lose a hot girl in a Swedish venue. You will not have a scarcity mentality.

You see, a girl's perceived value is relative to the place and situation. If you think: "she is more valuable because she is hotter," you will have a hard time adjusting to reality. A girl you deem hot in one bar might not even catch your attention in a hotter venue. So, if you don't want to be caught in the relativity of this concept you best not to think of it when you approach women. With this, I don't mean you will be approaching war pigs out there; but you must remove value judgements based exclusively on looks.

When You Look For Value Outside

When there are desirable things out there in your environment, you behave like a collector of value. You become a dog retriever, sniffing around, trying to get whatever you can. Then, when you do find something you value, you will bend over backwards to get it– the crossroads where external value searching turns into approval seeking. Because you realize that in order to get what you want, you must bypass your girl's resistance. Then you will need her approval. You need a "yes" from her.

> ## COACH DRILL
> ## Walk Like The Owner
>
> Destroy your validation or approval seeking by behaving like you own the club. Imagine people there are guests at your party. As a powerful visualization exercise, I ask my students to walk around the club for five minutes and try to minimize mental chatter and think they own the place. This has an amazing effect on their body language and general confidence. They relax, lay back and their shoulders become loose. They look at people in the eye and smile. Then, once they let go of external validation, I ask them to approach a girl right after they finish their walk. Then, you watch how relaxed and laid back they are as they talk to a female. They have removed approval seeking from their game in five minutes! Then again, perception is reality. If they perceive themselves as unique and all powerful, that's how people will perceive them. I keep going back to this drill many times in the night. As many times as needed.

With time, this habit of looking for value outside will turn into a nasty habit of approval or validation-seeking. You will need people to accept you or validate you to feel good about yourself. I cannot even begin to describe the devastating effects of validation-seeking to your progress because you depend on others to feel good about yourself. Others will control you. They will hold all the strings. Like a puppet, with no will of your own, you will feel disempowered.

Situational Confidence vs Core Confidence.
It Can Only Come from Inside

You can define core confidence as your Holy Grail. We strive for this. Core confidence doesn't depend on anything external like a skill, approval, or a situation. It comes from within. You act through your own intentions and you give approval to yourself regardless of whether you screw up or succeed. In other words, you don't need external proof of worthiness to feel good about yourself.

On the contrary, situational confidence comes from the situation, your skill levels, approval you get from people or anything external to you. In other words, if you were an accomplished lawyer and I were to ask you to give a conference to a group of law students in their freshman year, you would feel pretty confident coming into the lecture hall. You feel like you own these people since you have all the power that skill and experience give you.

Same thing if you threw a party in your back yard and invited all of your friends and colleagues. You wouldn't have any problems walking up and start a conversation with the hottest girl in your party. After all, she is your guest. Therefore, you will not be invested in approval seeking, you will laugh out loud and experience no fear of rejection on your own turf. The situation grants you reduced anxiety levels.

I want that same exact confidence in a club, away from your turf. You must develop situational confidence into core confidence in a club where you don't know anybody. I want you to repeat to yourself: "It is my house, this is my back yard," as you walk around talking to women. I want you thinking they are your guests who see you as their host.

The following effect will follow: when you are not looking for approval from people they will start trying to seek approval from you. They will give you undivided attention, laugh at your lame jokes, buy you drinks, etc. At times, girls buy drinks for my students on program nights. They don't want them to go away and bribe them with liquor. Reverse approval?

Stripped of everything self reliance (another name for core confidence) comes down to a strong sense of self that goes beyond your ability, the situation, the loud music, the people, and the chaos of a club. It comes from inside and not from outside. It is the holy grail of this game.

That's why some newbies can perform at the level of a seasoned veteran without either the skills nor a favourable situation. Their minds, un-invested in results, stop looking for approval outside and they become confident inside. It separates them from the average Joes (an army of needy, validation-seeking, approval seeking horny men), and therefore they are able to generate massive attraction. Women tend to fall for this type of super self-reliant men.

I asked myself this question in the last five years of instructing: Why can a newbie start a conversation on his first night of program and get mind blowing results, despite the fact he is doing his first ever approaches?

Say hello to an innovative industry-altering fundamental: core confidence.

How Do You See Yourself?
Can't Change The Fruit without Changing The Root

People perceive you as you perceive yourself. If you think you are awkward and a party pooper people will see that in you. And they will treat you in kind. It's the reason why you must think you are the coolest guy in the club and people are dying to talk to you. Visualize yourself walking up to people with a big smile on your face and making lots of friends. Hold that vision in your head as you walk up to strangers and turn them into friends. Don't crave approval from them but instead focus on having a good time yourself and talking to them. They will be glad to have somebody genuinely fun to be around.

Secondly, don't allow negativity to creep in. Focus on the positive. If you approach two people and one is receptive to you, choose to focus on the friendly one. Your subconscious will record that instance of success and retain it. It will soon be duplicated if you press on it.

> ### Reality Check
>
> *Don't fall into the trap of behavioural patterns. Back in the day, when I first started coaching, there was a trend of teaching guys "behaviours." Namely, an instructor would teach how to behave and not how to think. For example, guys would mimic an instructor's body language like sprawling on a chair with their feet on the table, occupying a lot of space with their bodies, being a jerk to women and so on. Most guys who did this didn't have the beliefs to support such a behavioural pattern. So they ended up faking it. We had all kinds of guys with jerk personas attached to a nerdy, geeky real self. They were out of sync with the behaviours they were displaying because they had nothing to back them up. You cannot sustain this long term. You can maintain it for a weekend under the close supervision of an approach coach but, once you leave the program, you will backslide into old behavioural patterns. Just like putting a band aid on a bleeding artery, your quick fix will not last. Bleeding will only stop for a while.*

I suggest you combine visualisation drills like the one offered earlier with the implementation of a strong set of beliefs like, "people are always friendly," and, "it is fun to approach." By doing this you will change the root of your tree in order to obtain a different fruit- can't grow apples from pear seeds.

In working from the bottom up, you will ensure those behaviour patterns are sustainable over long periods of time. If you neglect your belief system transformation, you will be stuck with your old behaviours. New behaviours will not be sustainable. A different reality will not be created.

To create a new reality you must sustain a behaviour for an extended period of time. This ritual will turn into something called character.

We want character-building in Pick Up, not unsustainable personality gimmicks. Your average players, after years of approaching women and substantial effort, force breed a character. They work the opposite way – from the branches down to the roots. Conversely, I want you to start working on character since you start as a rookie – right from the seed. You don't need years of approaching to build a set of principles to live by. You can't start embracing those principles today. Don't waste time.

CHAPTER 10

How To Become Fearless

*First Learn How To Remain unattached to outcome.
Become A Victor At Mastering The Process*

Competition

We live in an ultra competitive society. Seconds count. Text messaging, video conference, space tourism, you name it we got it. You turn on your TV and see Tiger Woods lifting yet another trophy followed by a word from a sponsor, who tries to pedal whatever, while replaying the Tiger's flawless performance on the golf course. The sponsor uses Tiger's perfect swing to sell the ultimate car, watch, etc.

We change the channel and what do we see. Whoah! Another winner: Federer winning Wimbledon and lifting yet another trophy, smile on his face while they replay in slow-mo his killer forehand. It looks like everybody's a winner.

But let's look at the loser. Let's look at Federer's opponent. He sits there waiting to be called for the Wimbledon's runner up's speech, with a look of resignation on his face, almost apologizing for being there. Even though he walks off with a cool million dollars in prize money – which makes him a winner in any economy in the world – he came second. What a shame. Down and defeated by society's high expectations he cries.

Well, in a society prejudiced against losing, coming second can feel worse than dying. People who die get more praise than a runner up.

But let's go back to Tiger Woods' swing. You can see how his body bends and his flawless stroke has the exact amount of force to drive the ball flying over the course for a perfect shot. Flawlessness incarnate. They sell perfection to you over and over as if they were telling you: "Be like Tiger Woods or you get nothing of life. Be perfect."

However, we are not sold on effort but on perfection itself. Furthermore, anything that takes time and effort gets frowned upon. Unless it's a product, a machine, a course that makes your life more comfortable in less time it stands no chance in the market place. Time and effort (required for any type of skill building and maturation) remain as outcasts, quasi-taboo concepts.

Needless to say, they don't show you how Tiger Woods developed his swing – because that would backfire. Advertisers don't care about the slow maturation of a skill building process: how Tiger started learning golf at the age of four or six with his father and developed his game patiently over time. Or how many days he practiced a week for the last 20 years of his life. They don't want to expose how many shots he missed or how bad his swing looked when he was a rookie.

That won't go in your average newsreel, for the public won't have the patience for it. Only Tiger lifting his trophy and opening the champagne will get through the countless layers of censors and editors in the newsroom. The public gets educated on these insane quick, no-effort-required values of our time. Somebody from another planet would not know what to think of us. A being from an alien civilization would get the opinion that we are reckless, irresponsible maniacs in the way we bombard our society with such images of perfection.

> ### Reality Check
>
> *Advertisers rely on images of perfection to sell their products. Those are the tools they use to create and maintain demand for their clients. But this perfectionist drive can sabotage us out of learning any skill.*

Why We Don't Get Good At Anything

We try to compete with the Tiger Woods and Federers of the world and we lose every time. Fixated on the bias against losing, we consider failure a horrible and sinister state of affairs.

As soon as losing rears its ugly head, negative thoughts kick in without much questioning. But negative thoughts have a quality of being pervasive. They won't go away. They keep haunting us to the point that we end up sabotaging ourselves out of a skill. We get lazy, stop practicing and quit. Discouraged because we will never be as good as Tiger Woods, we don't try golf. Why should I break my back practicing it if I am not going to make a million dollars of prize money in my lifetime? How can I compete with those guys? How can I compete with perfection?

Well, you can't.

Why Making Mistakes And Your Ego Don't Go Together

Our mind has a way of working that I find interesting – to say the least. We, after years of TV and media indoctrination, have grown to dislike failure and won't accept anything lower than number one. Whenever we can't achieve ultimate winning something we call ego rebels, throws a tantrum– the ripples of which affect us at a deep core level.

Your ego has a funny way of looking at the world. Unless you finish number one it tells you bad things. Your ego demands satisfaction all the time and its unlimited thirst for winning cannot be fulfilled in a lifetime. To be honest, I think you will be dying in your deathbed at the age of 90 from old age and your ego will be saying: "Why don't you die already and get it over with?" It has a tragic way of affecting our lives. Ego doesn't like failure at anything, even dying.

The Simple Truth In Learning Any Skill

More failures equal faster learning.

Like in all skill learning, trial and error lies at the heart of approaching women. Even though I can explain what needs to happen for a successful Pick Up, you still must go out and get it done. And you won't get it right away. You need to learn through your own mistakes. Coaches like me are there to guide you and give you motivation, but the ultimate responsibility to learn lies on the learner himself. The faster you go through your mistakes the speedier you will climb up your learning curve and become a master.

I like to give salsa-dancing examples because they illustrate my points better. I dance salsa as a hobby and I watch the best salsa dancers in the world on youtube. Now, I can tell you that even though I comprehend what needs to be done to pull off a beautiful move, it takes me lots of trial and error to incorporate a simple shuffle step into my salsa routine with my partner. A slow maturation process needs to happen first for your mind and your feet to work as a unit.

However, unlike dancing, you can make mistakes in Pick Up and still pull it off. You can come back from gross mistakes and salvage situations on the fly. Welcome empiricism in your practice and you will excel. Going through more impossible situations results in more learning.

Why Neither Success Nor Failure Are Real

Because they are not permanent states. They are both irrelevant in the big scheme of things. This becomes especially true in this game where they coexist all night. Every night you go out, you are going to have plenty of both – so much you will stop paying attention. You will educate your mind to be indifferent because it doesn't help you to think in those black and white terms.

You might find irony in this game: the girls that fancied you most when you first approached them won't sleep with you. Conversely, the girls who hate you at the beginning end up in your bed. Success and failure overlap when you approach women. You can suck all night and get laid with the last girl you approach. Conversely, you can get approval from girls all night but go home alone. You can also suck at approaching one group and have amazing success on the next and vice versa. At the end of the night, you won't remember much of it except for a few highlights.

Neither of the two states, success nor failure, will be forever. They all change and transform. Also, what you consider a success or a failure will change: newbies feel great if they can approach a hot girl and get a number; but advanced guys would feel bad with anything short of a lay, or at least a make out.

Ironically, you can have amazing success with the hottest girl in the venue at any given point, walk off and be told to go to hell on your next approach by the ugliest girl there.

Furthermore, when you are a full-blown veteran, if I can use that word, you will experience failure on a nightly basis. You will still fail to open some groups and take home girls. You may have had a threesome the night before (a striking success in anybody's book) and you are riding high on enthusiasm, only to find out the next day you can't approach a single girl standing idle in the middle of the club. When we feel on top of the world, we are most vulnerable to failing. Ups and downs should be considered an integral part of practice. Since they are not permanent, they must not be taken seriously.

Love Of Succeeding At Baseball.
Or, Why Childhood Examples Explain So Much

At the risk of sounding patronizing, I will give you a childish example. When I was a child, I loved playing baseball. I always was trying to get kids together to play in the afternoons after school. Although I wanted to win, I never thought of it. I did it for the game itself. I prepared everything, bat, balls, gathered the kids, and so on. The excitement of playing baseball was bigger than winning or losing. In fact, I don't remember if I won or lost any game in my childhood, I just remembered my enthusiasm for the game.

I did it for the sheer fun of playing: hitting the ball, running the bases, sharing with the other kids (the process). At that time I had no concept of winning or losing. No matter how the result of the previous game had gone, I was always excited to come back and play again the next afternoon. In our game, it can be counterproductive to go to a night venue with a fixed outcome (winning) in your head. Same way if you go the plate to hit a ball with any trace of an outcome in your head (getting a homerun, or a hit), you are doomed. The best hitters swing their bats to the tune of very simple mantras in their head like "Hit the ball hard, see the ball hit the ball. Get a good ball to hit." Going to the plate thinking, "I got to hit a homerun right now," can mean wasting a bat. Same with our Pick Up game: women will see through your intentions (Pick Up outcomes), and they will dismiss you for not being cool. Phone numbers, kiss closes, make outs, extractions will happen for you, provided you are chill, cool, lead physically and flow with your girl – the process. All this talk of process versus winning brings me to my next point.

But I Want To Win. I Want To Have Sex With Lots Of Girls

I hear you loud and clear. But I must warn you of the apparent paradoxes of this game. And I say apparent because they exist only on a superficial level. On the surface it looks like envisioning a goal in the field of play (clubs) will make you more driven, efficient and determined and get you what you want faster. But that's just the surface.

First of all, you must have goals or you will perish. Having said that, I must also point out that your goals must be process-oriented goals, not results-obsessed.

Let me explain.

My experience tells me a results-obsessed player makes lots of mistakes. Mistakes he can't come back from – like interaction killing mistakes or deal breakers. Very simple: as soon as woman sees you are trying hard to seduce her, she will run for the hills from you – with good reason, I might add. You are not an ideal candidate for sex or a relationship. You are just like the rest of the desperate guys who crowd the clubs any given Friday looking for a cheap thrill or a quickie. The desperate and needy get rejected on principle.

The Hairy Issue Of Agenda vs. The Fun – Or No Agenda Approach

Most people will be tempted to go in with a Pick Up agenda when they talk to a girl. You know, the usual: "First I open with my bullet proof opener, then I attract with enticing stories, then I hook-get her interested, then go into rapport, then get physical..." Most women will be repelled when they find out you have such an agenda.

They will think you are scheming with subtle games, tactics and lines to get her in the sack. They will be repelled by your pathetic attempts to get into her pants. I find no difference between doing this and buying her a drink to get her to talk to you – the usual MO of horny, needy guys.

Concealing The Pick Up Agenda

If you do go with a Pick Up agenda, you will be forced to conceal it. Then all your energy will be focused on preventing her from finding out you are trying to pick her up. Most guys fail to pull it off because they lack the long years of experience required to hide intentions and deceive people. But more importantly, you don't need to do that.

You must only change your approach to the game. I call it the "no agenda" approach or no "Pick Up agenda." You must strip your approach of weird Pick Up vibes because it will turn most women off and incidentally come across as needy, horny and desperate.

Conversely, my agenda, stripped of Pick Up, runs along the lines of finding out about her, getting to know her to see she is fun, having a genuine interest in her as a person. You might want her but you can't be attracted to her without knowing a bit about her first. You might like to be seen with a gorgeous woman but you don't know her. You don't know if she might be worth your time and effort yet. So, you approach her because you are curious.

I say have no agenda as you approach her. Let her sell herself to you. If she turns out to be a head case or a negative person or a bitch you will be turned off by her anyways. Ease into the approach and allow plenty of time to relax with her, don't be needy or tense, which are all deal breakers with women.

As a side benefit, since I have taught my no agenda approach, I notice students getting towards the end of the night with unlimited energy. Because they don't have to spend any fuel concealing their intentions and are just expressing who they are, they have access to untapped resources of energy in their bodies and mind. Before this no agenda approach, my students would show serious symptoms of tiredness and boredom two hours into the night in a club.

Today, as a direct consequence of having no burden of outcomes, they feel happier and loose throughout the program. On Sunday, our last day on program, you hear uncontrolled bursts of laughter and jokes all the time because of the amount of relaxation built up over the weekend. Approaching, once an anxiety-ridden chore, becomes pleasant and fun.

Alternatively You Can Have A Social Agenda Or Agenda Of Fun

With a public venue like a club, people go to meet people. So anybody can walk up to anybody and be social initially. If they don't like you, they can walk away. With free space to roam in a club, I am not forcing anybody to talk to me unless they want to. If they don't find me interesting, they can leave. If they stay, it means they want to get to know me. I must not apologize or find an excuse to talk to them. I don't need a reason. I am just being social and having fun.

Crawl Before You Walk

Random guys come on my program that want me to teach them how to get fast make outs, get one night stands, etc. They all want quick results like that. They couldn't care less how to get there. Most of those guys cannot open a single group of people or maintain a normal conversation with a girl, let alone kiss her. They want to close the deal before they can open. Cart before the horse.

On approaching you don't know what situation you are walking into. There are too many variables outside your control. First of all, nobody can guarantee your group will open up to you. Don't believe the fallacy that you can be such a master at this game that every group will open up right away to you. On the other hand, you don't know the fabric of your group when you walk in. They may be a group of girls on girl's night out, all of them married or with boyfriends. You might be walking up to a girl who has just sworn off relationships and men altogether. Alternatively, you might be walking up to a couple who happen to be there to enjoy the evening. The variables are so many we could fill paragraph after paragraph with situations I have encountered over years of approaching random people. So stop thinking you can control all situations.

Focus on the simple elements of the game like starting conversations and take it from there. You cannot control whether you will close your girl on your initial approach. It would pay not to focus on it and instead do first things first: approach her. Learn to approach with consistency, then move on to other more complex areas like making out, leading and taking girls home. Once you get a feel for opening, progress to adding physicality to your approach, then try to lead girls to the dance floor, etc... until you start making out. You can't fake real growth— you must pay your dues in time and patience.

What You Get Out Of An Interaction Is Not Under Your Control. So Why Focus On It?

Don't wrestle with the following paradox: "Results will come when you are not looking for them." Chasing results will make you needy and tense. People will run away from you like the wind. Nobody wants to be around a needy, tense, results-obsessed human being on a Friday night.

If you avoid the problem, you can have total command over your process, whereas, when you aim for results, you do not have 100 percent control. Things can happen. You have no grip over people's behaviours in a venue: a girl might blow you off; a guy might feel the need to mock you; the girl you made out with might have a boyfriend and leave shortly after, feeling guilty. Again, so many variables.

But you can always better your process. And that improvement has a powerful impact on the results you get. Because long time mental patterns die hard, newbies often experience anxiety about results. If you have just started going out, practice the following and you will soar like an eagle: After every group you open ask yourself "What did I do right?". Answer your own question. No matter how small or insignificant, if you did something well, make a mental note and describe to yourself everything you believe made you successful. Sooner rather than later you will be made aware of your own success patterns. You need to learn to spot success, not failure, so you position yourself in a unique position to reinforce it.

Like in any sport, you play to your strength and hope your weaknesses will come along. You trust your skills will show up when you need them and they do! That's why you need to stay positive and have fun. Then your best qualities will turn up.

Why Failing Big Will Help You Speed Up The Process

You must fail big to win big. If you are not succeeding enough you are not failing big enough. Outcome dependence cannot survive if you aim to fail high. To be a winner you must fail large and deep.

Your small failures will leave you more frustrated because you learned nothing. With no far reaching impact on your attitude everything at a small scale fails to ignite any fire in you. You walk into a group with low energy trying to sneak in their conversation, and the girls, feeling bad vibes from you, walk away with an excuse to go to the toilet. You feel like dirt. You behaved like a true loser. You cared too much about your outcome so it made you overcautious and reactive. Failing small will make you feel you are not committed enough to your process.

I would like to eliminate all your small failures. You want to fail big every time. You want large, deep and resounding failures. You need your mishaps to speak as loud as your successes and truly not care.

Screwing up will destroy the number one killer of interactions: trying to control the outcome of a conversation. People realize you are trying to get specific reactions out of them, so they know they can control you back in the way they react to you or what they say to you.

When you try to control the outcome, the outcome ends up controlling you. You fear you won't get the reactions you desire. You dread that things will end up messy. Finally, it becomes a self-fulfilling prophecy and your interactions go south.

If you have a controlling personality, this will be your number one problem. You will try to approach groups with a specific corollary in your head. When it doesn't happen for you, you will lose valuable time and motivation thinking about how to fix your approach. However, nothing is broken, but your Obsessive behaviour. It's an exercise in futility. You can't bridle events in human interactions. Chips will fall where they may. In accepting randomness, you will find your freedom from outcome.

You can only get a grip on the process. Like I said before, there are too many variables not under your direct influence – a losing game. After failing in a big manner for a while, your control-obsessed behaviours will be shattered and you will enter a new realm in your game – the realm of outcomelessness and practice for the sake of practice. You will grow stronger inside. You will become a resilient player with a healthy ego.

I Tell My Students To Go And Try To Have a Big Fat Failure

I want them to go and get hardcore blown out by girls. I lower the bar for success at failure level. I instruct them: "Go and get rejected and I will give you a high-five." But they can't. It turns out the more they try to fail, the more they succeed. Go figure.

Again, I don't know why trying to fail has a positive impact on my students' games. I am not very much interested in whys. I am more into what works. It seems to work to let go of outcome dependence. As it happens, you can benefit by not walking into a group with a particular winning or get the girl agenda. Stripped of a preordained seduction frame up, guys relax around women and do their best work.

What's The Path Of Being Un-reactive?

Nothing new here, I am teaching something which has been around in every sport or skill-oriented activity for years. We just started applying being un-reactive to Pick Up. Nothing exotic in it. It's rather ordinary if you look at the world of sports.

Take baseball or tennis. Players learn not to react to the last event, rather flow with it. In other words, you must become un-reactive to the events in the game if you are to keep yourself in the game. Andre Agassi – coming out of retirement– learned not to be affected by the last point played in the match (like the last group you approach in Pick Up) whether good or bad. He learned to focus on the point in hand (here and now, like the group of people you are approaching). He went on to make one of the biggest comebacks in the history of tennis at an older age. Barry Bonds, the player with most homeruns in baseball ever, says he doesn't aim to "hit a home run"(outcome oriented, reactive thinking), but to "look for a good pitch to hit"(process oriented). All major league sluggers when asked say, "homeruns happen". But they don't look for them. At the plate they focus on being relaxed and they let the bat do the talking. They train hard (a difficult process), but they play easy. Similarly, getting laid is something that just happens in Pick up.

My osteopath instructs me to "let go" in order to ease the pressure on my injured back (a gym injury). For some reason, I can't do that. I must "reprogram" myself to relax my muscles. But again he instructs me: "Stop trying." Amazing. Sounds like woowoo, but you can find this philosophy everywhere now. In every performance-oriented activity you must learn that in order to "perform" you must be calm and not tense. Why do some people cringe when I say they should be chilling and releasing their tension around a girl and stop trying to Pick Up? Obviously, they haven't woken up and smelled the coffee of up-to-date performance-related coaching.

Why A Do-Or-Die Attitude Won't Work

After all I have explained, you will still go out and try hard at succeeding. You will wrestle your way into a lay. And let me tell you, you might get it right at times. Meaning, if you are hard enough on yourself and break enough eggshells, you will end up with girls. But why all the trouble, when you can choose the path of un-reactiveness and join the group of successful people who focus on the process?

I have mentioned George Leonard and his book *Mastery*. In it, he explains the way of the master. Namely, how masters at any discipline share a simple common trait: they all love to practice. They all excel because they enjoy the process of training. They love to roll up their sleeves and do the work.

In this game, to relish your practice means having a good time out in a club with things under your control: approaching women, pulling them onto the dance floor after a quick conversation, going for kiss, etc. Like I say to my students, you need to welcome even your rejections: a girl dismisses you and you walk off with a big smile on your face like she made a joke. You must rise above the obstacles in your way by not getting involved.

The road of goalless practice and surrendering to process not to your outcome will make you a healthy player— one who stays in the game for the long haul, who is flexible and unbreakable. You want to become one of those solid, consistent guys who go about his practice naturally and effortlessly.

The Threshold Of Indifference

If you are to succeed, you must cultivate an attitude around the game. You need to nurse an indifferent concern to results – yet another paradox. Such a lukewarm approach will keep you in the game through the rough times and level you when you are having jaw-dropping successes. In other words, it will keep you sane and keep your head in the game.

The highs and lows kill the regular player. Don't be a regular player. Be the resilient, outstanding, consistent player. I cannot even begin to describe what happens to typical players without flinching with pain. Average players get on extreme highs when they accomplish something and sink to severe lows when things go down the toilet. Most of these guys suffer when they lose a girl at the end of a night after a four hour make out session. They thought she was in the bag, but she wasn't. They go home and rack their brains about what went wrong. 99 percent of the time nothing went wrong, just the unpredictable nature of this activity.

Good Nights And Bad Nights

Since no activity can yield a constant string of successes, and lows are both necessary and predictable, you must stop grading nights into "good" or "bad." Walk out of the club after four hours of Pick Up with a stupid grin on your face, like you just had a blow job in the toilet. I don't care if you nailed the club DJ's girlfriend and made out with her behind the DJ's booth, or you got rejected by the fattest hippo woman in the club. You must remain level and understand nights can go either way.

In the same vein, you must stop labelling interactions as "good" or "bad" for this will also kill you. You will feel bad when interactions suck and good when they go well. Very soon you will be fishing for "good interactions" only, which will kill your flow and spontaneity. Stop labelling things as good or bad and you will save yourself a lot of trouble. All interactions are good anyway because you had the balls to approach in the first place.

The Inner Tension That Results From The I Must Pick Her Up Now Mentality

You are standing around in a club and you see a girl or a group of girls and you go: "I must go and pick her/them up now." This performance dependent thought carries a lot of tension attached to it – tension that will be transferred to your interaction. You don't want to be walking up to women with such tension in your belly. They will see through you.

So what should go through your head? You might want to develop your own working agenda. Personally, I see a girl (or girls) and I think, "I want to find out who she/they is/are," or, "I want to go and have a little fun with her/them first." That seems to ease the pressure and makes me more relaxed on my approach. Rather than thinking, "I must perform now", I tell myself positive and uplifting things that put me in the right mind frame to approach. Girls perceive me as nonchalant, extroverted, fun-loving rather than stressed out, manipulating or conning. In addition, I feel myself honest and authentic. No downside.

Process Oriented Goals?

The be-all-end-all solution? Yes and no. Without result-oriented goals we have no direction. You want long term goals (one month goals, three month goals, etc.) in your game. You should measure progress by pure, stone-cold factual results at the end of a period of time (a week, a month or a year). Yet on any given night you want to be as process oriented as you can be. You will have plenty of time at the end of your month to revise your goals, reset them or celebrate when you get them.

But tonight, in the venue, you are about the process – how to get there. You need to put all your faith in the process and it will take care of results. And do not panic when you don't get immediate success.

I use the question of how I can make their nights better. This process is my goal when I approach. I make sure I offer or add something to the vibe of the group. I want to leave them better than I found them. Other times, I repeat to myself, "Bring some joy into their lives."

Though this might sound cheesy, esoteric or woo-woo, it has a tremendous effect on my enjoying the process. It makes me feel extremely valuable to them and to anybody. Again, we are after what works for you. These little mantras help my game. You need to find the ones that help you the most.

Another successful process oriented goal I have used on my program is to get one girl on the dance floor in the first 30 minutes of approaching. This seems to get a guy's mind off the end game. As a result, most guys end up with two or three girls on the dance floor. By the end of the night, they drag four or six females onto the dance floor instead of one. They excel because I give them goals related to the process of Pick Up – not the end result. Later on, we will discuss (See Chapter 11: High Energy Game) how bringing girls onto the dance floor can help improve your kiss-closing ratios.

Feel Like You Have A Ton Of Value To Offer

Have you helped anybody looking for directions?

If you live in London, hundreds of lost tourists run into you asking for directions. It even becomes annoying, I might add. But in London, as in most cities, if you approach people for directions, they go out of their way to help out. You see how good they feel helping you even though you are a stranger, and you won't pay them for it. Have you ever felt good helping somebody? If you haven't you are not human.

I will tell you a story that illustrates my point.

We were approaching random women on the street during one of my daytime sessions in London and my student approached a two-girl group that was looking for the right tube to catch. He helped them for a while by going around the underground station like crazy, looking for the right tube line. At the end, one of the girls asked him to go with her to a summer festival she was attending that afternoon. Voila! Just by helping her. I asked my student about how he felt when he was helping her find the right tube line. "I felt good inside, like I was doing something without an ulterior motive in it," he said.

That's how you should feel when you talk to people. It should feel right. It should feel not as if you are doing something to manipulate them but that you are enjoying talking to them. Being process oriented rather than results dependent, was required in a girl asking the student to go with her on an instant date. This is the beauty of not caring for the outcome of an interaction.

Keeping Things Moving Forward vs. Having An End in Mind

Faith in the process gets stronger when things are going dandy. However, you need to have faith when things don't go as planned. When I work the field I keep things moving forward rather than having a specific end in mind. This type of mentality helps me get through the night whenever I get stuck or I don't seem to be getting anything.

I use "churning the cream for butter" as a metaphor to describe this process. When you churn cream, you beat and beat, and no butter comes out for a long while. You keep churning and it seems like you are not getting butter at all. Like a pie in the oven half way through the baking, it looks bad because everything looks imperfect in the middle. But you keep churning the cream and eventually you get butter. By working through those weak moments, where you feel like giving up, you will get nice butter out of cream. Meaning you will hit it off with a group of girls, or a single one, and everything will go smoothly – to the point you won't remember the bad moments at all.

I feel like letting the cat out of the bag. What if I told you, I have the technique that will destroy all your outcome dependence? In the next section, I will tell you of a simple technique guaranteed to put you in process mode. This technique will not only ensure you that will not be result dependent, but it will also get you out of a jam. It will get you back in your game.

Ready! Here we go!

Lower The Bar!

When you lower the bar, you can always jump it. Simple! Do this and you will always excel. Permanent winner. Big smile on your face every time because you will always be ahead of the curve. Personally, I like to lower my bar as far as I can when I am in a club. Knowing myself to be an Obsessive type, I push the bar down as far as I can so I can feel good no matter what happens.

I say to myself: "I showed up at the club, I am a winner." You see the value of this? The criteria for success have been lowered so I can finish first. When I enter the club, regardless of what happens, I already won the game – I showed up. Many guys choose to stay home and watch TV and jerk off to porn. I am a winner because I decided to step out of my comfort zone and be at a club talking to real women. It feels great to do something for yourself. Having such a fun, positive attitude helps me when I approach groups because I project it on to others.

I use the following drill with students when they get stuck because of having too high expectations – and the pressure they generate. This drill, a development of the lowering the bar concept, has saved plenty of guys in the field when they are struggling.

COACH DRILL
Five-in-five

Introduce yourself to five girls in five minutes, making sure that the last girl should be the hottest in the group. Variations include hugging five in five minutes, and high-fiving in five minutes. These drills succeed because they are done fast. So they don't allow you to think about what you are doing. Forget picking her up as you do this. I have found with five in five drills, when the smoke settles, guys end up talking to one of the five girls for the next hour. It works.

A Drill That Will Change Your Life!

Ok. I am in a super good mood and I have decided to give away a huge part of my program here. You will love it. I will give you my centrepiece drill for destroying outcome dependence in my students. Feel free to use in a similar environment.

I loosely call this exercise "Surviving a Crappy Opener," – an all time favourite with my clients. They cannot stop raving about it after they have done it.

In it, I put you in a situation where you have a 99 percent impossible chance to get an outcome. And I make you repeat the seemingly losing routine over and over until you start enjoying the process, not for the outcome (getting a girl) but for the sake of it. This drill has proved over and over to have amazing results in shaking the "results dependence" out of every guy.

> COACH DRILL
> **Surviving-A-Crappy-Opener**
>
> Get in front of a girl in the escalator at the tube, open with a "Crappy Opener" and try to change the topic. You only have until the end of the escalator to do this. You can open with something silly like: "Is Hyde Park a real park?" Or: "Is Buckingham Palace a real palace?" Or directions: "Where is Victoria Station?" – while being in Victoria Station itself. Then try to change the thread of the conversation. On an average, you have a couple of minutes to do this until the end of escalator. Then, you are supposed to leave the girl and come back down using the adjacent escalator. Then up again with the next girl and down again. I guarantee after 30 minutes of doing this you will start noticing how you chill out, how you stop looking for an outcome and start talking to people for real. You will see a smile coming naturally in your face as outcome orientation slips away from you. It's very eye opening indeed because no matter what you do you know you will lose the girl at the end of the escalator.

Something mind-boggling starts to happen during the course of this little drill: as you let go of controlling the outcome, more and more girls stop at the end of the escalator and start a conversation with you. Only because you seem like a socially-calibrated, cool guy with whom it's good to hang out. After walking up and down the escalator for a while, program students start to dig up gold and end up taking phone numbers and getting instant dates for the night...

To win a lot, you must lose a lot. In the beginning, it will look sloppy. But there will be lots of girls down the road that will jump at the opportunity of being with you. You must believe that focussing on the process instead of the outcome can save you from numerous pitfalls and landmines in the game.

Ozzie

Focusing on the process by being indifferent to the outcome is one of the best-kept secrets of over-achievers. Most successful people will mouth about their goals or dreams – but when it comes to getting down to business they are all about the process. Aiming at the ritual itself, not the consequence of it, will give you a sure shot at getting what you want out of life. As you focus on the how, you forget about the when and the what. You get sucked in by the moment and let go of your concerns. Feel free to use the above drills to practice freedom from outcome.

Part Five:
Closing The Deal And Trouble Shooting

CHAPTER 11

High Energy Game

*Prime Mental State For Physical Game. How To Get There.
Approaching On The Dance Floor And Building A Leading Frame*

People Reflect Your Energy Levels

First of all, people mirror everything you are doing and are affected by how you feel. So if you have low energy levels when you approach a group of women who are having fun, you will suck away all their enjoyment. In other words, they will feel you are bringing them down. They will resent you for it and blow you out. Nobody wants to be around a leech.

For starters, you must be a source of good feelings. The buck stops with you. In order to provide good feelings, you must feel them first – you need to get excited.

By being the provider of positive energy, you will own people's reality – you will suck them into your world. If you don't, you will find yourself reacting to them. However, I don't want you to get the idea you must entertain people (I will deal with the entertainer type later); rather I want you to communicate positive feelings to your environment at all times.

How High Energy Should I Be?

High as a kite! Not really. Most people imagine high energy means bouncing up and down around the venue. However, what's high for one guy means low for another. For an introverted type on my program, a really shy dude, I would say: "Go super high," and he would just put a smile on his face. That's high for him. On the other hand, if I have a super enthusiastic positive guy on program, who is all excited about talking to women, I might say to him: "Go and bore the hell out of her."

Then, he would approach with a clean and positive vibe. It would be an overkill to say to that guy: "Go and be high energy."

In other words, not high, not low, just have the type of energy you would like others to have around you. Do you want people to be friendly around you? Get friendly. Do you want people to be positive around you? Get positive. It doesn't get any simpler. Put out the kind of vibe you want from them. They will mirror it back to you.

> *Reality Check*
>
> *Being negative around people tends to bring out the worst in them. You don't want to be going around telling stories of how your doggie died of leukaemia. People will feel sorry for you, but they will resent you for destroying their mood on a Friday night.*

The Secret To Maintaining Your Energy

Here it goes... Ready?

Eat and sleep before you go out.

Due to going out three or four nights a week, many guys neglect eating and sleeping – only to find themselves without any zest after an hour of talking to women in a club. Have a meal before you go out because you will need the fuel. Guys enter a night venue on an empty stomach and complain later they lost 'state' (a jargon word for zest, energy, attitude, mental fitness). If you don't eat, your body has nothing to work with, so your reserve energy supplies will be depleted in no time.

Sleep can also determine your power supply levels. I make sure I have a nap on Saturday before going on my second night of program. It always helps. I feel I have more energy towards the end than anybody else. I cannot stress enough the importance of being on a high when everybody else in the club is winding down. Most people towards the end of the night, because of alcohol and wild partying, tend to drop their energy levels. You will be at the top of your faculties and awareness when theirs take a hit. You can work your extra supply to your advantage.

I advise my students to get on some kind of exercise multi-meal program. I eat five to six meals a day plus I go in a church-like fashion to the gym for my five-day-a-week workout program. I kid you not when I say you need this if you are serious about Pick Up. If you plan to burn the candle at both ends in the clubs you might as well prepare. Going out four to five nights a week takes an immense physical toll. If you neglect your fitness you will find yourself struggling two or three months down the road.

Can Music Help Put Me In Good Energy Mode?

I have heard listening to your favourite music before going out helps build up positive energy inside of you. Elite athletes listen to their favourite songs before they have to perform. I used to listen to my favourite CDs in the car on my way to the club, but today I use the music I have on my phone. However, I fail to a see a far-reaching impact on my state beyond enjoying music I like.

Still, I recommend dancing in the club to the music in any way you can. I use this when my students are feeling uncomfortable. I take them onto the dance-floor and we do some crazy dancing. After a while (say, three to five minutes), I ask them the golden question: "How comfortable are on a scale of one to 10?"

If he answers any lower than six, I keep dancing and repeat the question every three minutes. Once I hear a six or a seven, we resume approaching women. Dancing gets your mind off approaching for a while. It gets you out of your head. But you must resume approaching as soon as possible; otherwise, dancing becomes another avoidance mechanism to help you stay in your comfort zone. You don't have to be an eight or a nine to start approaching again. A mere six will do.

Change Your Physicality, Change Your Mind

Because most people feel a rush of high energy through their body after running a 100 meter dash as fast as they can, I started to use running in clubs too. I ask my students to jump up and down with me for a while in the middle of the club. If they don't have the energy levels required for approaching, I ask them to run through the club. The combination of social pressure – (lots of strangers watching) with the rush of physical energy from running makes them go into high energy. They release adrenaline that can be re-channelled into approaching women. It never fails.

COACH DRILL
"Slap-My-Ass"

When my students are struggling I use this simple drill: I ask them to do something awkward until they get back into an optimal state. This drill will put you into 9 out of 10 in comfort level in less than five minutes. The exercise consists of going to the dance floor and trying to get in the middle of a group of girls, where everybody can see you. Then you shake your ass to the girls and do not say a word. Rattle your behind in such a way that it would embarrass every human being in the planet. Go nuts. You do this until you get a girl to slap your ass. You are not allowed to talk to them until you get your goal – a girl slapping your ass. Don't worry if you freak girls out in your first couple of attempts, as you should power through all kinds of rejection, while amusing yourself. This drill requires you to have fun doing it yourself rather than entertaining them. You are not their entertainer. You are doing this for you.

A Secret To Getting Into A Positive State That Works 100 Percent Of The Time

Ready? Here it goes! Get somebody else in positive state.

You will fail to get another person in state unless you are in a positive mood first. So as you try and change your friend's state, you will change yours. I instruct my students to get me in a good state on my programs. I pretend I am in a sorry mood by looking down at the floor, pretending to be sad, so they must get me back into state fit for approaching girls. As he tries to lift me up into happy state, the student himself gets all pumped in the process.

If you are going at it alone, pick a group of girls in a night club, and get them jumping up and down. Make it so you get them to feel happy. In turn, you will get happy. Try to avoid entertaining them because that will defeat your purpose. This group of girls that you made cheerful will become what I have come to define as 'state pumping stations'; namely, a group of girls I befriend with zero intention of picking them up, who I will come back to every time my energy is running low. They are my zest pumping station. I sometimes have two or three pumping pit stops in a venue. I come back to for a refill of good positive energy throughout my night. By being proactive and thinking way ahead of time, it goes without saying that I often end up hooking up with one girl from such groups. Results happen when you are not looking for them.

Why Friendly Game?

I make my students befriend an entire room of people on the first 30 minutes of my program in a venue. By removing their thoughts about outcome (picking up girls) and making them approach people just to be friendly, I have found their energy levels skyrocket. After a while of befriending the room they are in such a great state of mind they are ready to do anything and everything. It turns out that removing your goal from an activity makes it more enjoyable. It helps guys to focus on process rather than being obsessed with a specific end.

I use this friendly technique on-and-off throughout my program. I call it: "Taking a step back." Every time my students struggle in the field, I instruct them to take one step back and focus only on befriending the room. As soon as I see they've got back into their stride, I push them to grab girls and go for the make out. I have experimented a lot with removing outcome from interactions and it never fails to amaze me how well a guy can perform, once you remove any expectations from the table.

Do this: every time you are bogged down because you are not getting what you want in a club, be goofy for a while! Approach people and say things like: "I love you guys," or: "I want to be your friend."

Do it playfully but genuinely.

Because of the hard ego stretch, being goofy will put you right into a great mood. You will not believe you were able to behave in such a friendly manner. Keep going goofy until you get a feeling your inner resistance has lifted. Then, go back to whatever you were doing.

Having Fun Must Be The Goal of Your Interactions

You can fake fun by doing something called entertaining. But people will sense your duplicity right away and get defensive. By trying to put on an act to make them like you so you can get what you want, you turn into a dancing monkey or entertainer type for them. People can spot this from miles away. Some guys, unaware of what they are doing, turn into smooth-tongued approaching robots geared to please the public. In their minds, the more positive reactions you get, the better off you are. However, the energy cost of running a show for others will make you pay a hefty toll.

Genuine fun means liking yourself regardless. You will find the more you like yourself, the more others like you. You can't fool people on this. You must have fun when talking to others – enjoying interactions without the duplicity of wanting anything back. When you do this, it will feel effortless, like you are not carrying water for them. They win and you win. Most people approach this game in a win/lose mentality. I must win so the girl loses. Girls are your enemy to beat, conquer, and pillage. Think instead if you both meet and you both had fun with your interaction, even if it didn't lead to sex, you both won. This win/win mentality will keep you positive and healthy inside.

When You Are Running A Show. Energy Depletion

There are two reasons why a guy runs out of energy too early in my programs. Oftentimes, both operate on the same guy. Firstly, he forgot to eat/and/or sleep that day or he is not fit physically. This game requires a lot of physical energy from you. You need to eat/sleep well and go to the gym to be in good condition. With a minimum four-hour marathon of talking to people on three to four consecutive nights, you pay a toll with your body. You must be proactive about this and get on a gym and onto a multiple-meal eating program, aside from hitting the sack like a hibernating bear during the day to make up for lost night sleep. If you are serious about getting good at this, you must make some changes in your life style.

Second reason (which I am quick to spot and stop): they are running a show. They are performing, so it takes all their energy to keep their show on the road. They have found early in the night that they can make strangers stop and listen to them for a while if they entertain them, the way a performer would, but instead of magic tricks and clown-painted faces, they are using conversation.

Since they are not trained artists, the stress of running this show can make them pay a huge vigour tax. They go bankrupt energy-wise. After a while they stop trying. It overwhelms them. I hear entertainers take years to develop 15-to-30 minutes of solid material for their show. My guys pretty soon find out how hard life can be in the show business. They run out of entertaining things to say and find themselves ejected out of a lot of groups.

Entertaining And Controlling

You can define entertaining as a controlling behaviour, an exchange: you give them entertainment and in return you want approval. However, people's reactions are outside your control. There are too many variables involved. When you try to control things out of your reach (like people's behaviours and actions) people end up controlling you. Namely, when they give you approval you feel good, but when they don't, you lose motivation. Craving their attention and acceptance becomes your energy's silent killer.

You can patch this up with what I like to call zero expectation. Expect nothing from them. Don't read anything into their reactions to you. Don't attach meaning to their opinions of you. Don't look at people as a source of validation. You need to be entertained from inside, not outside. Validate yourself, your story, your values, and your life first, and then talk to people without searching for their consent. Easier said than done. You must pay your dues by rehearsing it over and over when you approach. A conscious effort at first, with time and practice, it will become second nature to let go of people's approval. You cannot fake any real growth – you must pay the price.

Dance Floor Game And High Energy

It took me a while to figure what I did on the dance floor. It was not until many of my students tried to imitate me and failed – and, then, I tried to help them get it right that it hit me: in trying to explain to others what gave me results, I became conscious. I started to break down something I did in my flow state.

My dance floor game was developed out of sheer improvisation. Its benefits are many – but I must single out fast make-outs as the juiciest of them all. However, I must warn you, fast make outs don't represent solid game – but they do get you to first base.

I kid you not, I have made out with girls in seconds on the dance floor to the astonishment of my students and myself! Students always say the same thing, "I could never do that." Yes, you could! If you had the iron balls to try it. It's very important when you go for quick closes not to have any approach anxiety and to be in the moment and having genuine fun. No cheating there. Half-hearted approaches will get you blown out.

At a club, I am the guy having all the fun – huge smile, dancing all the time, jumping up and down, with an irresistible fun vibe. So much energy, it would drain you to just watch me. I do that to the point girls ask me the question, "What are you on?". Then, I tell them to get a sip from my drink of choice: water or soda. And then I go: "You just ingested a cocktail of high calibre drugs" "Do you feel it?", And they go: "Yeahhhh!!!" Funny.

I do have lots of fun doing dance floor approaches because I love music and dancing. However, I will tell you a more compelling reason to get in the habit of pulling girls on the dance floor...

The Dance-Floor As A Shortcut To Getting Physical

The dance floor offers you every excuse to jump into physical escalation under the pretence that you are just dancing. If she likes you, she will welcome this opportunity to get closer to you. Even if she didn't want you at first, she might start thinking about you as a potential suitor if are able to grind with her in a confident manner. This works because the dance floor gives you isolation – one-on-one time with her away from her friends and the social pressure of her peer group. By freeing her from the enquiring eyes of her friends, you give her the chance to act on her real feelings toward you. Alternatively, if she doesn't like you, it gives you a unique chance to change her mind.

I have often witnessed a girl giving a lot of resistance to a guy, even being rude, until the guy pulls her by the hand on the dance floor in a nonchalant fashion, without talking too much, and then five minutes later they are making out like crazy. This tells you how powerful Physical Game can be at changing her emotions. All your physical leads such as grabbing, spinning, and grinding can skyrocket a girl's attraction to you in no time.

> *Reality Check*
>
> *Be aware of dance-floor-monkey syndrome. When you are with a girl on the dance floor you will find it easier to stay in your comfort zone and not pull the trigger. You might both even be having fun, but nothing happens. I practice salsa dancing and you see this all the time in all salsa dance floors: as soon as the song finishes and you stop dancing, your girl walks away and you lose her. Alternatively, a girl might stay a whole night with a guy because he can dance. In both cases, they put you in the "friend zone" and never give you serious consideration as a potential sexual partner. You become the dance partner for the night. To patch this, either you pull your trigger and go for the make out or yank her off the dance-floor, and try to start a normal conversation with her outside of it.*

Do I Need To Dance Well?

I hope you become the type of guy in the field bent on opportunity not on crisis or problems. I have been with plenty of both types in the field. An opportunity minded guy proves lethal in terms of results. He uses everything to his advantage. Wide open for kissing, the dance floor offers a perfect opportunity for physical escalation. And, in addition, you can "pump her state"(jargon word for getting her excited or pumped up with adrenaline) by dancing with her. Once she gets into that optimal fun state, you can move in and kiss her. You will find far less resistance this way.

No need to be a pro dancer, not even a need to be good at it; I have taught simple dance moves to guys who had two left feet. I teach them a basic move like putting their feet together and separate them (opening and closing), and then we try to follow the beat that way. We start bouncing and that's it. They are ready to approach girls and pull them onto the dance floor. If you don't believe me, take a look at the guys on the dance floor. You will see they are monkeying around and bouncing, but they can't dance. However, you see them grinding girls and making out with them too.

Simple moves like spinning can be easy and full of possibilities. For example, you start dancing with her, extend your hand and grab hers and then spin her. Sometimes, I have used this to kiss her. When she turns, I pull her towards me and go for the make out as I spin her around to face me. Sometimes, it is that simple.

Leading Her Back And Forth From Her Group To The Dance Floor

I do this all the time. I bring her to the dance-floor to dance, and then drag her back to friends. I instruct my students to keep doing this throughout the night. And then attempt to make out in one of those trips to the dance floor to seal the deal.

This tactic prevents the group from getting uneasy and starting to look for their friend. If you don't bring her back often, they will send a scout to find you. If they suspect their friend has been kidnapped they will cock block you. They do this as pack behaviour– a way of looking out for each other. They know their friend gets drunk in clubs and ends up sleeping with a guy, and then complaining about how she loses her head in clubs.

So they will send somebody to see whether she is all right. Many times I have had a girl dragged away from me after making out with her because I didn't bring her back often enough. I prevent this by leading her back from the dance floor several times to her friends. This pays high dividends at the end of the night when you make your final move to take your girl home with you. If they trust you, because you didn't steal the girl from them, they will even encourage your girl to go home with you.

Moreover, by moving your girl back and forth from her peer group you create an illusion of a date. Resembling a courtship, you are taking her to different parts of the venue with you. In her mind, she sees herself following you and you leading her. It reinforces the idea of a romantic outing where you do things together, plus it helps you set the leading frame necessary to pull your girl out of the club.

When the time comes to take her home, you have moved her around the club so much that you have built in her the habit of following you around. In other words, she trusts you. You take her home as your final lead. Many guys fail at the last minute because they haven't established this all-important leading frame. Because they haven't moved their girl around, a follower's habit in the girl hasn't been formed. So when they say to her, "Let's go home," at the end of the night, they haven't built any trust in their lead. Girl turns hesitant or flat out resistant to the idea of following a guy out of the club.

I make a habit of leading. I have pulled girls from clubs to a restaurant and when they sit on the chair they drop. They are exhausted. I have moved them around the venue so much their heads are spinning. I must admit I have exaggerated my leading because I would rather have a lot of leading than lack of it. So I overdo it and I exhaust my girl in the process. You can never have too much leading.

Approaching On The Dance Floor

You follow the same principles when you approach on the dance floor. Yet there are certain things that are different. For example, people's mental state on the dance-floor rises due to the dancing – they get pumped up. So if you approach them with low levels of energy there they won't even pay attention to you.

So you must pump yourself up first. Dance to the music, slip into a high energy state – which for some could mean putting a big smile on their face, and for others, it could mean jumping up and down like a maniac. If you are a natural high energy guy, you won't have to do much since you are already excited. Don't overkill it.

Ozzie

To get yourself excited forget outcome for a while. Don't think Pick Up when you are on the dance floor, only think in terms of fun and games. It has to be fun for you first. Outcome orientation to get results will push you to low energy levels, which will render you ineffective in such a high energy environment. Play around, clown and jump up and down – anything other than Pick Up. The majority of guys, subdued by the power of quick results, will start second-guessing themselves if they don't get a make out within 10 minutes of approaching on the dance floor. So, instead, try not to think of quick results when you approach. Focus on fun.

Secondly, once you are in a flow state, find the most excited and pumped up group on the dance floor and attempt to merge with them. If the girls are dancing, approach sideways while dancing yourself. Then, try and bump hips with them. Alternatively, you can knock together buttocks while back-to-back, which I find very effective. It seems safe for them to touch bottoms with a guy.

Once you got a girl bumping hips or bottoms with you, you must take it easy and not rush into grinding. Just let both of you get comfortable dancing with each other. Once you achieve comfort, try and talk to her by getting closer. This will allow for further physical escalation such as putting your hand over her shoulder in The Claw position. Once you lock her with The Claw keep alternating between talking (barely saying anything, just introducing yourself – don't talk much, you are on the dance floor!) and grinding.

Moreover, keep your escalation moving forward until you go for a make out. Don't stall too much because moods on the dance floor go pretty high but come down with the same amazing speed.

COACH DRILL

I see dance floor approaching as an opportunity to test the student's stamina to rejection and help him build a thick skin to a girl's emotions. Every now and again I bring a student onto the dance floor, make him approach there, then take him back to a quieter area. His approaching skills outside of the dance floor improve sometimes to an all time high. Equipped with the energy, pep, and stamina developed on the dance floor, he can approach effortlessly outside of it. It has a powerful effect on his game.

The Physical Game

Most guys attempt to approach all night without becoming solid approaching machines. I believe most action is distraction – 20 percent of your actions account for 80 percent of your results. Most people fail to take the right kind of action. 20 minutes of approaching on the dance-floor, under a high energy, seemingly hostile and difficult environment, make a guy solid when he steps out into a calmer environment. 20 percent of the time on the dance floor will account for 80 percent of your results outside of it. The old 20-80 success rule proves applicable to this game too.

Do The Rules For Starting Conversations Apply To The Dance Floor?

Yes. You must enter your group by kicking the door down as opposed to sneaking in. If you sneak in, you will be thrown out. Your levels of energy must match theirs. That's why I recommend first approaching the group on the dance floor that is having the most fun. It will be impossible not to be contaminated by their positive fun. From that moment on, it will be easy to approach by kicking the door down, because you will be carrying with you a lot of momentum from that very group.

Try and engage the whole group the same way you would outside the dance floor. Of course, you won't be able to talk to them as a group because the music will be too loud at times. I take guys to parts of the dance floor situated right under the speakers because I want to challenge them. Despite the noise, try to pay attention and dance with every one of your girls in your group, one or two at a time. This way everybody in your group will know you are not a predator for sex or a needy guy. Don't worry about delaying talking to the girl you want in your group, you will get to her in due time. As a top priority, you must share your fun with them as a whole and have a party.

Do Physical Game Guidelines Still Apply To Dance-Floor Game?

Yes, they do. Get physical right away and keep escalating. A typical mistake would be to just dance far away from your girl, because you are afraid that if you get too close, she will blow you out. The distance between you and her will tip her off if you are either too uncomfortable or too predatory by sizing her up.

All these signs coming from you will make her suspicious of your intentions. She will sense duplicity in your approach. She will get defensive and you will get rejected. Your only agenda as you approach must be genuine fun. If they sense an agenda, they will run. On the dance-floor women have a far-reaching radar for horny behaviour. Be mindful. You can be pigeonholed as one of many drunken guys trying to get lucky.

Instead, approach with confidence. Dance with her and get close to her fast and amplify your physical escalation by means of high-fives, hip bumps, bottom bumping, hugging, and spinning. All of these moves should be done close to her body without giving off vibes you are testing the waters. A predatory attitude will tip them off to the fact that you are uncomfortable. Of course, you need to repeat this over and over until you find yourself having genuine fun with groups of girls – the empiric approach. Expect lots of rejection and lots of fun doing it.

The Don'ts Of Dance Floor Game

I am only going to give you your basic ones. Many things can go wrong on the dance floor because people go there to lose control. However, I have seen certain behaviours you want to avoid because they will reduce your chances to zero. For example, never hover around a group of girls while trying to muster the courage to approach. They will see you in their peripheral vision and you will be blown out. By hovering around you are stalking them. You will trigger all kinds of red flags. You will be rejected on principle.

Low energy level is another *Don't*. You stand no chance with this one. By approaching with a low level of energy you will become an energy sucker. You will suck the fun out of them. You will bring them down to your level. To curb this, before you approach, get into some kind of high energy state by dancing, jumping and doing something silly. Alternatively, you can use some of the drills I have suggested before.

Passivity can also keep you from success. For example, a guy approaches a group of girls with ease, engages them all and he goes passive. He stands there and stops engaging the group. Most of those guys think: "My job is done." They think that way because they were able to approach and get the interaction going. Now they can sit back and wait for the girls to jump onto their penises. Of course, such a thing never happens and they find themselves doing nothing in the middle of a group of dancing, screaming, crazy girls. As he stands there passive, girls start to think he is not fun after all. His initial "fun guy" impression was just a facade, a front. They perceive duplicity and get defensive.

Dance-Floor Conclusion

Use the dance-floor to take things to the next level: getting make-outs, physical, etc. It can be a very powerful weapon in closing the deal. However, you must look at it as a tool, not as the meat of your practice. By this I mean, don't go to the club and spend your whole night dancing. Don't be dance floor-dependent. Go to a club, do your approaches, and use the dance-floor to close your deal – or simply to get yourself up into optimal state.

CHAPTER 12
Loud Music, Bitches And Rejection: Frustration In The Game

*Learn The Reasons For Frustration On A Night Out.
Understand Why A Business Approach Will Not Fly In A Night Club.
And Some New Solutions to Old Problems*

Disappointed?

In this chapter, I will dig into the roots of disappointment when you practice this game. I think the true cause behind frustration can be found outside the game, in the real world.

Something I call the measuring system accounts for most of our disappointments growing up. At home, your parents measure you – whether you are "doing well," or, "you are a disappointment." Same when you get a job. A boss evaluates you – or worse – the marketplace. In our culture we are measured and made to feel bad if we don't live up to somebody's expectations. Our lives are a constant struggle not to disappoint. Because we are so used to being evaluated all the time, we become entrapped in perpetual disappointment. Most of our social conditioning comes from this elusive, but obvious rating system. We don't question this scheme. We are born, grow and die in it without questioning its validity. Most of this assessing comes from people who in turn are being measured... And so it goes all the way to infinity. Then we come to the game. And what do we do? Same old measuring. Saddled with outcome dependence, many guys cannot let go of their measuring. Good set/Bad set? Good night/Bad night? Good opener/Bad opener? Good/Bad performance? Good Pick Up school Vs. Bad Pick Up school? Good advice Vs. Bad advice? And the list goes on and on.

Find The Courage To Be Imperfect

My best performances when interacting with girls have been flawed ones. I came back from gross mistakes or salvaged hopeless situations. Then, results came tumbling in. How imperfect you allow yourself to be defines your level of courage. How much of a risk are you willing to take? How much measuring can you let go of? On live infield programs guys struggle with the old yardstick embedded in the depths of their brains. Unable to accept Pick Up as a discipline based on empiricism, most guys are terrified about making mistakes. Why? You guessed it right: the measuring system. They dread being rated bad. It destroys a guy's natural ability and coolness. Because he can't relax he can't perform. His own outcome oriented mind paralyzes him. The confidence comes from outside. It needs positive feedback from the environment to live on. So it is not real confidence because it depends on outside factors like a girl's approval. Guys need to be reassured even when they *are* doing right. An external supervising agent must validate their performance.

In order to bypass your dictatorial self rating system, I recommend you go by the following philosophy:

PPT (Practice, Patience and Time)

1. *Practice comes first*
   You won't improve if you don't practice live, i.e., approach girls. No book, DVD, or seminar will give you what practicing in the field will provide. Just like on writing courses where they teach the mantra "a writer writes," so in Pick Up, we interact live with women, with an emphasis on approaching. (The internet game is still comfort zone game in my book.)
2. *Patience*
   Without patience practice turns into hogwash. You will abandon things at your first mistake or the second. Without patience, practice becomes useless. You will open a couple of groups and hang by the bar because you don't see progress. With trial and error at the heart of building your skill, no patience leads to inconsistent results.

3. *Time*
    You need to take a lot of time to practice. You must schedule your practice or you will not train. For example, I will go out Fridays and Saturdays rain or shine. That way, I arrange my life style around my schedule, not the other way around.

Then, don't judge results on the basis of good or bad. Stick to your PPT game plan no matter what the results are. Don't go black and white on your progress. You need to shelve your yardstick because you grade out of compulsion, not common sense. Understand you are ok as you are. Progress will happen anyway if you apply the *PPT* philosophy.

Negative Self Talk And Frustration

It has been said a child hears the word "no" several thousand times more than the word "yes." Since we are raised in a negative and prohibitive society we are bombarded with phrases like: "Don't...Not possible...You can't," as we grow up. Geared towards making us social (another word for live by the rules conform, obey orders), most societal programming has an apparently harmless quality. There's nothing wrong with living by the rules, and society needs a certain amount of no's to be called civilized. Otherwise it would be a jungle. However, by enforcing these rules in young children, side effects like negative thought loops can be created – otherwise called negative filters.

For some people, "no" type of thoughts become the only thoughts. Our brain produces around 20000 thoughts a day. If you have a negative filter, and you only process the negative as a side effect of the above-mentioned social programming, your brain can only focus on garbage.

People with negative filters can only stay on negative thoughts. They project, aggrandize and live by them. Due to the constant probing of this discipline, those people will focus only on their failures. However, unless you mess up here and there, you will not learn to approach women the right way. It's similar to learning to ride a bike: you fall off many times and you get back on it until you ride away.

In this game, since it is far more painful than falling from the bike, rejection deters guys. They focus on it. At the end of a program night you ask a student if he remembers three things he did well, and he has to juggle his memory to retrieve a couple of isolated instances where he succeeded. Some, those with strong negative filters, can only relate their mistakes.

When I remind them of the things they did well, they respond: "I guess I did that too. It was ok." Their negative filters don't allow them to focus on the positive. On the contrary, they fix on the negative. Needless to say, such a fixation can damage your game. It destroys your capacity to learn.

Learning Styles And Their Far Reaching Impact

In Chapter 6, I described the learning styles according to George Leonard's insightful book, *Mastery*. When I coach Pick Up, I make it a priority to make my students aware of their particular learning style— for in awareness lies the cure. Once you know the hidden forces at work you can do something about them.

Like I said before, these learning styles (Dabbler, Obsessive, Hacker) will deflect you away from your mastery learning curve. If you look at a prototype learning graph you can see how plateaus are 80 percent of it and climaxes account for little or nothing. It means a master spends most of his time ploughing his way through level ground.

However, due to their learning styles, students of Pick Up will suffer and sometimes quit in the middle of a plateau, when they don't see things happening or climactic moments. Let's say you hit your club at 10 pm and nothing happens for half an hour. You talk to girls but it doesn't feel like your best day. You hit a plateau. Nothing you can do, but keep working and don't panic. If you get frustrated you might sabotage the rest of your day's practice. You must learn to love plateaus as a symbol of good things to come. You must change the way you look at your game in order to become consistent. Take those plateaus as a sign that you are on the mastery curve and you are on your way. Level stretches come with the territory of solid practice.

The Two Most Common Learning Styles In Pick Up

The Obsessive and the Dabbler are the two most common learning styles. If you are not an Obsessive, then you are a Dabbler. If you are not sure, you may be a mix of the two. However, don't be fooled: one style owns you. It might take you some time to identify it but, once you do, the practice of Pick Up becomes simpler– because you will be able to spot your own tendencies and correct them faster.

If you have trouble classifying your learning style, take a look at totally unrelated activities like sports, job, and hobbies. If you have started four new hobbies in the last year, and didn't stick to any of them, you might be a Dabbler.

Your pattern shows in every area of your life – to the point that I have even spotted my own pattern (Obsessive) in relationships. Then again, you might show a different pattern depending on the area of your life. For example, you can be a Dabbler at learning the guitar (you practice it on and off, but never take it seriously) but an Obsessive in your job (always worried about perfection and not screwing up).

From my experiences teaching Pick Up for five years, I know 80 percent of students are either Dabblers or Obsessives or a combination of both. The rest, 20 percent, are Hackers. I am going to focus on the two most important ones – the 80 percent – and how to deal with those two patterns.

The Catch-22 Cycle Of the Obsessive

An Obsessive sports the mentality "I want it now" like a nametag. If an outcome doesn't come to him, he suffers instant frustration. I have seen guys get frustrated after 20 minutes of cold approaching. They cannot take it anymore. Being a reformed Obsessive myself, I feel for those guys. They give up before they have even started.

Unless they see tangible results in the very short term they cannot enjoy their process. Because of his obsession with the end goal, an Obsessive cannot enjoy practice. A lack of instant results causes him to dislike the process – talking to people, that is. And since you cannot communicate with people effectively when you are in a bad mood, this leads to ever-increasing rate of underperformance. With less motivation to practice, you end up with a sub-par performance, which leads to further heartache – a vicious cycle or Catch-22 of sorts. An almost unbreakable pattern if you are in denial.

Your average Obsessive, aside from being too outcome dependent, is also rigid in his view of the world. In his mind, a certain amount of effort must yield a proportionate amount of results. However, this proves to be wrong for any skill that requires a lot of trial and error before you get any type of payback.

In the world of skills learning, you might sometimes work for long stretches without seeing anything proportionate to the amount of effort you are putting in. Like in the gym, if you want to build muscle, you must work hard for the first six weeks and see no muscle, only pain. It doesn't mean you should stop. Your body is transitioning and adapting.

Apart from enjoying your process as an Obsessive, you need to drop self-criticism to zero. Having an overly critical eye on your actions will render you useless in less than an hour. Obsessive types seem to be ever self-assessing themselves. But with self-assessment most guys evaluate down instead of up. They always grade low in their assessments because their expectations are too high. For example, they tend to have a criterion for success that is impossible to meet like: "Every girl must like me," or: "I must have three make outs within the first 30 minutes of approaching or else I suck." With this tyrannical self-critic inside your head you don't stand a chance in a club full of unpredictable circumstances. Flexibility, stamina, and a positive attitude are required to triumph.

The Novelty Chaser. Meet The Dabbler

As George Leonard explains in his excellent book, *Mastery*, a Dabbler starts practicing a skill for the thrill of it. As soon as the novelty wears off, he moves on to a newer activity that can provide fresh excitement. Having no follow through capacity, a Dabbler starts learning many things, but never finishes any of them.

For example, those people who say they speak six different languages *started* six different language courses, but never learnt any of them well. Professionally, Dabblers have long résumés. They change jobs every six months because they get bored and want to move on.

You can recognize a Dabbler in Pick Up without much effort. After 30 minutes of approaching women, the novelty loses its initial lure for him and he starts getting bored. As the fun runs out in a repetitive activity, he tries to finish approaches by ejecting out of conversations as soon as he encounters a bit of resistance.

He ends up "bouncing"(a term we use to describe a guy's inability to get deeper into conversations, which results in rapid fire interactions) from one group to the other like a ping pong ball. In a hurry to finish, he approaches an entire room full of people in less than 30 minutes. It means his approaches average two to three minutes. He can't stand the repetitive nature of approaching and ploughing through rejection.

To attack the dabbling pattern, I use the mantra: "Burn interactions to the ground." Meaning I don't allow a student to leave the group until he makes out with his girl or gets blown out. If he does eject early, I will send him back into the same group he just came from – my Peñalty to Dabblers.

Once I make them go back a couple of times to the same girls they just walked out on, their interactions start to get longer. Going back to the same group proves more uncomfortable than to hang in.

Years after they have taken a program with me I meet with such students, now successful in their dating lives, and they all tell me the same thing: "The only reason I talked to girls was because I knew you were there behind me and you would send me back again." Afterwards, with my authority replaced by their own, they become self-disciplined without any help. They become their own teachers.

Self-sabotage

Self-sabotage can be defined as a self inflicted defeat. You might not believe it, but some people want to fail. I have heard poker pros say that when they play a big hand they look for somebody at the table who wants to lose. Pros maintain that when the pressure goes up, because of the large sums of money at stake, you can find a player at the table looking to get rid of his/her money. He can't stand the pressure and wants to lose all his money. So a smart poker player will try and spot the player betting to lose. Though it's hard to believe, you must respect the pros' assessment.

In Pick Up, you can identify self-sabotage in a guy who is rejected by every group he approaches. By failing fast, he ends the torture of approaching. To win requires too much responsibility so he chooses to get blown out as the easy way out of a jam. Bad habits that would tip you off about self inflicted failure include talking to women in a low tone of voice (sucking their energy), not pushing the interaction forward when you find resistance, ejecting early, and standing in the middle of group in a passive manner.

Far too common to be overlooked, self-sabotage can creep up on the way you approach groups; therefore, you must have an eye out for wanting to fail to avoid responsibility. If you find excuses to leave groups early without making a serious effort to engage them, then this tricky pattern might have a hold on you.

What's The Victim Mentality In Pick Up?

When you play the victim, you look at your world and blame people for how bad you have it. You say others are doing you in. In the same way, you may find all kinds of victim patterns in guys trying to get good at Pick Up. Have you ever heard guys saying, "women are all bitches"? And you have probably said it yourself in frustration after something went wrong on the approach. You might react in anger towards a girl who has wronged you on the approach. Males tend to look outside for causes of problems. We never believe the real cause lies inside of us.

I have heard over the years the same old tune many times from rejected guys: "Women are bitchy in this club." However, on a closer inspection, I see other guys in the same venue talking to women and they seem to be hitting it off. What do they have that the angry guys don't? Well, I will tell you. For starters, they don't have victim mentality.

Every time you point a finger to something (bitchy females, music too loud, over crowded venue, etc.) outside of yourself for your lack of success, remember that there are three fingers pointing back at you –the real culprit. People who blame things outside themselves for their problems are trying to stay as they are. They just want to lay back and let things remain the same. So if you single out anything in your environment to blame for blowing things, you may be trying to stay unsuccessful – because making an effort to succeed will involve taking a hard look at the real smoking gun – you. No effort is required to kick back and blame the world.

> *Reality Check*
>
> *Guys love playing the victim so they don't have to take responsibility for their actions. After a rejection, "she is a bitch" thoughts can invade your head-space. Especially if you are addicted to blaming people for your problems. You must realize in all likelihood your approach to the girl was to blame for her rejection, not her.*

Failure Related To The "I Am Going To Get Laid Tonight" Attitude

Have you ever heard guys saying: "Let's go out and get laid"? But they never do. On the other hand, guys go out and get laid all the time without trying too hard. Coincidentally, if you look back at the times you got laid, it was when you were having fun, and were not on a mission to get pussy. Therefore, it pays to go out hunting for fun instead of sex.

You will find too much outcome dependence which will create tension and neediness inside of you. Because of their advanced radar for horny guys women will detect such things and they will reject you on principle. You must find a reason to go out other than to find a sexual partner for this tactic to work. The "I am going to get laid tonight" attitude only serves to scare women away. You must not misunderstand me because I have been talking of getting physical quickly, leading girls, and pulling them home. However, in no way meaning that sex should become an obsession.

A healthy indifference to results should be used in place of a head on collision approach to females. Needing an outcome to feel good about yourself will sabotage you when you talk to women. People will get defensive when they perceive you are trying to control them.

Interactions will end up controlling you – rather than you controlling interactions. Tools for your game like getting physical, leading, and pulling girls home are great servants, but horrible masters. Don't let the outcome of your game become your master.

Back Sliding. The Weekend Warrior

Most guys are weekend warriors in Pick Up. That means they go out on weekends and try their best to hone down their approaching skills.

But sooner rather than later, the issue of consistency rears its ugly head.

It doesn't work if you put on your caped superhero costume at weekends, but during the week you are more like Clark Kent. It worked for Superman because of his super powers – but won't for you. In order for you to become consistent, all behaviours, beliefs, attitudes should be reinforced during the day-to-day. You must become well-rounded. An exterior paint job for your weekends-only won't work. Behaviours like approval seeking, neediness, horniness and passivity must disappear and inner beliefs (like: "I am good enough...", "I am likable and lovable...", "I can get girls...") must be honed at all times.

It means you need to apply the principles that are going to make you successful in your game to every area of your life. That's why you hear so much talk of self-transformation and identity level change among practitioners of Pick Up. They realize that to try this stuff only as a weekend hobby can have little or no yield.

In order to change your sex life, you must change your life first, much like if you want to lose significant weight, you must alter your lifestyle. No short cut there, but long term commitment. Reversal to old patterns will be waiting around the corner, unless you enforce what you learn in your game on a day-to-day basis. Things like taking risks, pushing through resistance, being yourself around people, are all new habits and principles to live by. You need to become yourself.

Resistance To Change – Or Homeostasis

After a couple of nights out, maybe a couple of weeks on from your new readjustment in attitudes and behaviours, resistance will kick in. You might find yourself backsliding into your old behaviour of not approaching women and leaning against the bar. Don't panic at this predictable pattern. Let's analyse it in detail and give you strategies to deal with something called homeostasis – or resistance to change.

Homeostasis keeps all systems balanced and doesn't know whether your changes are for good or bad. Homeostasis doesn't know you have been without a sexual partner for years – even all your life. Your Homeostasis thermostat guards the balance in your body. Anything that threatens balance and it will go off sending alarm signals to your brain. It will tell you to stop. More than telling, it will yell, scream, shout, itch, and kick at you. A rebel force will descend upon you.

I like gym examples because they illustrate things well. I have been running for two months now, using intervals on the treadmill. I use intervals of higher and lower speeds to shock and awe my body whenever it reaches balance point. I go high intensity for a while, and then drop to lower, and back to high.

However, in two months, I never went higher than the 12th level of speed in my treadmill. 12 can push me to jog fast. I must switch to long strides that are of a different quality to the shorter strides. It takes a mental and physical stretch to go 12. Then, I decided to go at 14 speed. That's only two points above my max. Shouldn't be a problem, right? Wrong. As soon as I switched to 14, I started to run out of breath.

But I kept increasing the time I spent on this dreadful 14 by going back to 12 and climbing to 14 at intervals. It went from one to two minutes, then three minutes... Man, I sweated like a pig. I was puffing and panting for air. As I finished my 25 minutes cardio session, every part of my body was screaming for help. Please, stop, it seemed to say.

Ignore the pain? No. "Let pain be your guide," professional body builders advice you. If it's painful, take one step back. Regroup and reduce intensity. Then take two steps forward. Go faster again. Keep negotiating resistance back and forth like this and you will be golden.

Goals will be reached and passed. Negotiating resistance with your body will take you all your way to wherever you want to go.

Like you might have guessed already, my new comfort zone plateaus at 14 now. Yes! 12 looks like a walk in the park now.

Let's say we readjust thermostats to a new level, a new habit and we commit to it. Your new habit might be, for example, talking to women all the time you are in the club. You might find yourself doing that for your first night, and be happy with it for a while. But resistance might stir sooner rather than later and you will back slide into being idle by the bar. You turn back to an old behaviour of standing around and watching other guys Pick Up girls. Old familiar behaviours brought on by homeostasis sent you into the comfort of passivity.

Don't panic. Recognize your old behaviour and kick the new into gear as soon as you can. Accelerate and start approaching women all over again. Don't wait too long or you will get cold feet. Ignore inner resistance and plough through until you build your new comfort zone around talking to females.

Today, I can't stand around idle in a club without talking to females. I am not comfortable unless I approach.

> ### Reality Check
>
> *What is back sliding? You can define back sliding as a regression to old patterns. We implement a new behaviour for a while through repetition and sheer power of will only to find ourselves reverting to old patterns after a while. Since the new conduct has no solid ground, the old can pull you with relative ease. You cannot avoid this process. We thus find ourselves going back to comfort zones we thought we had left behind. Tilting back happens to the best of us. You must be prepared and willing to deal with it as soon as it appears if you want to succeed.*

The "I Am Going To Die" Signal

This signal activates a powerful resistance, namely: you would rather have your nose caught in a door than push the interaction to your next level. Your afore mentioned thermostats send a distress signal to your brain in the form of a false alarm. On change overdrive your thermostat deems it unsafe to keep going forward.

For example, this all too recognizable "I am going to die signal" flares up if you jump on your treadmill and crank up your speed when you are out of shape. You will find yourself panting and gasping for air in less than 10 minutes of running. Your brain will demand that you stop. Marathon runners advise against listening to such signals and to keep going and dismiss it as non-life threatening. After awhile your body adjusts to your new speed and you will have a great cardio session. You sweat and burn more calories this way. Next time, you crank up your speed, you will find less and less resistance until your body thermostats adjust themselves to your new speed.

The same happens in Pick Up when we do something out of our comfort zone, like approaching a big group, a mixed group (guys and girls), or go for the kiss close. Your brain will send you death threat type signals. But as you ignore them and keep going, just like on the treadmill, these signals tend to disappear— and that means you succeeded at readjusting your inner thermostats. Not being alarmed by such distress messages coming from your body will allow you to go further than you thought you could in the game. Train yourself to spot and ignore those moments of inner resistance and you will do fine.

If You Are A Success In Other Areas Of Your Life...

... It can hurt you. Yes, you heard it. Be aware of trying to become an instant success in Pick Up. The clubs are full of the ghosts of guys who thought they could apply their business principles and succeed. Unlike in a business, you won't make transactions here. With neither accounts to balance nor a bottom line to honour, you are better off not approaching Pick Up the way you go about a commercial enterprise. It can backfire.

I have trained many guys who claimed talking to a group of girls should be no problem because they had done successful business presentations for thousands of people. Others claim they have great people skills in their jobs and they can motivate entire teams to great heights of corporate achievement – so, approaching women in a night club should be a piece of cake.

Nothing could be further from the truth.

While all of those achievements are great, these very people find themselves struggling as they approach a bunch of boozed up girls dancing like maniacs in the middle of the dance floor. With these guys, I send them on suicidal approaching missions on purpose. I want them to find out straight away that Pick Up bears no resemblance to a business meeting. High flying CEOs fear rejection just like the next guy.

Most of these guys put the same pressure to succeed in Pick Up that they carry into their business. They start trying to control the outcome of interactions – only to find interactions start controlling them. Their added pressure to succeed with girls makes them too invested into approval seeking, or over tense; in turn people get defensive and don't open up to them.

If you are stressed out in a business way, people will refuse to talk to you. They have enough pressure from their jobs and they can't be bothered in their down time. So you can understand why they will blow out a guy with a "game face" on. By trying to impress them with your business savvy you just push them away.

I would like to finish with a magic pill for the stressed out. You might not like it at first, but, like a good medicine, it tastes bad but gets the job done.

COACH DRILL

I use this drill with guys who are trying to impress people or tip the outcome of interactions on their favour. I give them a simple mission: "Go and bore." I want them to walk up to a girl and bore the life out of her. I want them to let go of their need to entertain, impress, and be smart or funny or articulate. I want them to feel free to fatigue her with their talk. My student must approach and say something like: "Hi, I woke up in the morning, brushed my teeth, went to the office, checked my mail. I rarely have any breakfast..." And so on.

Now if the guy walks out of the group and the girls are all giggly, I tell my student I am disappointed. He hasn't accomplished the goal of wearing them down. So I send him to another girl in an attempt to give her a boring conversation. I instruct: "You must tell her where you live, what you do, how many brothers you have, what kind of car you drive, and etc." In other words make her yawn.

Because girls feel the guy is relaxed and not trying to get a reaction out of them, they want to be around him. The previously-stressed guy ends up talking to a girl for an hour with this drill. With no pressure to succeed, guys ease into interactions.

CHAPTER 13
Closing The Deal And Extractions

Learn What The Masters Of Getting Laid Do. Adopt The Core Philosophy Of ABP - Always Be Pulling. Discover How You Don't Need To Bring The Girl Home To Have Sex With Her. And So Much More...

Why Play the Game: Finish What You Started

Why play this game if you don't take girls for sex? We want to get laid. We want to have abundance of sex in our lives so we can make choices about the women we want. If you don't have such abundance, you are still in step one, no matter how well you pull off other parts of the game, such as starting conversations, being yourself around girls, getting physical, and so on.

As nice as it sounds, to be able start conversations with women anywhere doesn't mean you are living in milk and honey land. If you don't have multiple sexual partners, you will be weak. Though plenty of guys can approach and talk the Pick Up talk, only a chosen few can pull the trigger and bring a girl home.

Abundance means having too many women in your life to the point that you get phone calls for sex all the time. Having enough means turning down sex to go out and practice the game on any given night.

To get there, you need to close the deal with a lot of girls. You need to become a closing machine. And I want you to make closing fun for you. I will dedicate the next few pages to walking you through what it takes to become a closer in the game.

What Does Being A Closer Mean?

In general, we refer to closers as guys who get laid a lot. They seal the deal with regularity. However, to give you a more accurate picture, closers seem to do certain things on a consistent basis that make them successful.

A guy who gets phone numbers, pulls girls out of a club to another venue or home, isolates girls from groups, attempts to go for the make out, and gets physical fast, will more often than not be considered a Closer. If you try those things, time and again, you will become a Closer over time. Unlike a technique or a trick you pull out of your sleeve, you finish the job out of habit. It means you become a Closer. You don't gimmick it.

Why You Will Be Wasting Your Time

Throughout my practice, I have heard the same complaint time and time again: "I can approach girls now, but I am not getting laid." That griping can be heard like a pop song that refuses to go away in Pick Up circles. Guys get good at having meaningless interactions with women, but can't pull the trigger. Some of them can get phone numbers out of girls with ease; even make girls like them. Yet they have no pulling power. No power to cut through the bullshit and lead the girl home.

On closer inspection, you will notice that 90 percent of those guys are terrified of getting physical with girls. Interactions run a chatty course and end up nowhere. Having no physical component, the conversation goes south because girls lose interest. She can't wait forever for the guy to make a move. For anything to happen, you need to take risks. You need to jump in the pool with the cold water. Let's see how we can accomplish that from the start.

Starting At the End. Start Closing Early

Because guys end up stalling their interactions, meaning they pass up every opportunity to get physical due to fear of rejection, I started teaching them to get physical from the start regardless of approval.

At first, I taught clients different handshakes, high-fives and hugs. I would instruct students to take every opportunity they had to get physical. For example, shake hands and keep the handshake going for a long time, after she has introduced herself to you. But I found it more effective to teach physical escalation: from the hand shake, pull her into you and put your other arm around her shoulders. Do this without a real reason. If she says she comes from Germany, high-five her and tell her you love people from Germany – even hug her for it. In other words, take every opportunity to get physical.

It worked well, but I was not quite there yet.

Physical Lead

Failure to lead the girl physically will create a vacuum of leadership in the interaction which will be filled by her – meaning she will decide what to talk about and what to do. That's the last thing we want, because it will result in the girl getting bored and disqualifying you as a potential candidate for sex.

Rather, I want you to take each and every opportunity to establish a strong physical leading frame. I want you to grab her hand and spin her. Use The Claw on the opposite shoulder and dominate her that way. Last, but not least, you must tow her away from the group onto the dance-floor. All these things will reinforce the idea that you are in charge, not her. That's the key to becoming a Closer.

All guys who do this on a regular basis end up with make outs, kisses, pulling girls home at the end of the night or with solid phone numbers. Verbal game in itself pales in comparison to the power of steering a woman physically.

And remember, when leading, never ask, just take. Don't ask her to go to the dance-floor to dance. Instead, lead her there by saying: "I want to dance now". Coupled that with pulling her by the hand in a firm manner. Expect resistance and deal with it. Most girls will put up some form of front at the beginning of the interaction. 9 out 10 times such defensiveness is token, not real. That's why you must acknowledge it and plough through. Never give up. Take the rejection if you must, but get in the habit of leading her, regardless of her reaction.

> **COACH DRILL**
>
> Step into a group of girls, and within two minutes of starting your conversation, grab a girl by the legs with both arms and lift her up in the air like a trophy. Alternatively, if you are a strong dude, put her on your back and walk away with her. Disregard resistance and repeat the action plan until you get them giggling every time. This exercise will destroy the myth that you cannot get physical right away. Plus, in doing something so radical and far out of your comfort zone, you will gain a lot of confidence to perform less challenging stunts like hugging them, high-fiving them, and pulling them onto the dance floor.

How To Kiss Close

I must be honest and say I have flunked at teaching how to kiss a girl. I have tried everything from teaching students to sneak the kiss by telling the girl to close her eyes (childish, right?) to cunning enticing Pick Up lines like: "On a scale from 1 to 10 how much of a good kisser are you?" (Suave, right?)

However, I hit the nail on the head when I stopped teaching how-to altogether. My students made out with more girls when I started teaching them to get physical with girls from the start and disregard whether they approved of it or not, than with any other technique.

It would be difficult to transition from pure verbal game with no physical contact to a kiss. Women will reject you on principle because they need to be comfortable with your touch. As a natural progression, things get heated up as you apply different physical techniques before going for the kiss. It will not be forced because you both have been physical with each other and she grew comfortable with you touching her.

> **Reality Check**
>
> *Most kiss close lines and attempts fail because of lack of the physical component in the interaction. The guy has been talking "yada, yada" for one hour. His physical contact has been weak. He has trusted in his verbal skills to get the entire job done and then he gets blown out when he attempts to kiss. This is a natural reaction since he hasn't done anything to warm her up. They have just been talking. Any physical advance after a long period of passivity will be viewed as awkward, out of place.*

With no other short-cut but getting physical, you must simply go for the kiss. I, however, recommend taking her away from friends for maximum yield. Without social or peer pressure, she will follow her true emotions towards you. Separating her from her peer group, say, onto the dance-floor, will require a strong physical lead. You must become a leader. That's why guys with lack of a physical lead don't end up with significant make outs or kiss closes.

Once you got her away from friends on the dance-floor (or into another area of the club), it rests on your shoulders to amp up your physical escalation. You need to spin her, hug her, high-five her, and get lots of body-to-body contact by grinding, using The Claw or any other physical technique I have discussed earlier.

Once you have laid the groundwork, you need to go for the kiss. How? Well, just go for it. Let's say you are grinding on the dance floor, lean forward and go for it. No preparation, or technique required. Alternatively, say something in her ear and go from the ear to the mouth for the kiss close – simple. Your only requirement is to have had lots of physical game prior. She must have gone through the grind of physical escalation before kissing you.

When the dust settles, you will end up with a lot of lays and make outs.

Most of my second nights of program look like dance-floor programs. I instruct students to get every girl on the dance-floor and escalate things there. By the sixth girl on the dance-floor, students start to make-out. Others don't need so many. Some make out with the first girl they bring onto the dance-floor. You must consider here the randomness of outcomes in this game.

Word of caution: if you are pulling six girls onto the dance floor every night and not getting any kiss closes, chances are you are not being physical enough from the start. Failure to close on the dance floor indicates you are not physically leading girls prior to taking them there. It means you do very little aside from saying, "Let's go dance." Most girls go with you because they want to dance not because they are attracted to you.

A Story

Once I had a student who would go for the make out within 10 minutes of meeting girls. Just like that. Most people thought he was crazy, but he wasn't. He ended up with a lot of make-outs per night. His M.O. was that he would approach and grab the girl, put The Claw aggressively on her shoulder and talk to her from a very close distance.

Once he got her in this position, arm on her shoulder, body-to-body contact, he would go for the kiss after five minutes just by saying: "You are sexy, I want to kiss you." That's it. That was all his game. He got lots of rejections, of course, but he got lots of make outs and lots of lays under his belt. He made me rethink my whole approach to the game.

You could be inspired by watching him do his thing, namely, making out and dumping girls for hotter ones and not giving a damn about the outcome at all. That stuff doesn't happen out of the blue. He made it happen. In my opinion, he found a way to reduce game to the bare essentials, to its simplest form: either she gets down with him or she has to find a way out of his grip and run – because he won't.

The expert runs an autopilot screening program for women: either they get with his program or they must find a way out of it. From what he does when he meets women, far reaching lessons ensue. He is experimenting with hardcore physical escalation and seeing how much he can get away with. He can have a lot of fun because he views his interactions with females from a learning stand-point. Every night he apprehends new lessons about how far he can get in the shortest amount of time.

He is pushing the limits of reality. By going through all kinds of rejections, he forces himself into great epiphanies. Once the dust settles, after months of practice, he will end up with lots of make outs and lots of lays under his belt. He will find himself enlightened.

To shrink your learning your curve, you must start doing things that seem uncomfortable first, but become your new comfort zones over time.

Why Getting The Cheek Is Not A Bad Thing

I once had Dutch guy on my program who went for the kiss 11 times and got the cheek instead – but created an obsession.

I know most guys would have given up after a couple of attempts. They would feel they are wasting their time and move on to the next girl.

Well, this girl in particular, even though she never kissed my Dutch student back, got obsessed with him. She hung on to him like a clam. She would not let go of him even when he tried to move on to other girls. It looked as though she was attached to him like a Siamese twin. She refused to separate. She wanted him, but she would not kiss him.

Even after we ditched her (we had to move on with our approaching program for the night), she started stalking us around the club. She would stand behind us. She danced around us trying to get our attention. She butted in our conversation many times. She would not let go.

Lesson learned. You could interpret dodging your attempt to kiss her as a sign you screwed up, but nothing is further from the truth. Good things happen after this apparent rejection.

Despite the seeming failure of getting the cheek, you succeed at making the statement that you want her. In spite of her rejection, you further communicated to the girl that you are serious about her and you won't give up. All these traits of courage, persistence, and manliness elicit strong attraction in females. They are all desirable qualities in a man. They are universal and most women will fall for them.

So the next time a girl gives you the cheek, think nothing of it and try it again. See it as a plus not a setback. Most guys are shaken by such rejection but players love this, because they have stated their intent to get her. Now she knows you want her for more than friendly talk. The ice has been broken and the ball is in her court. Next thing you must do, try it again – the three magic words of Pick Up. How long? How long can you do it? It is up to you. Like I say on program: "If she is still there, do it again."

Why Being Persistent Pays

I would say go for the make out or kiss close a minimum of three times –based on my theory, women cannot say "no" more than three times. Run the train and keep running it and ignore token resistance. Girls are programmed to put some kind of front to your advances, and if you don't persist you will never find out if she fancies you. Some people call this "testing," meaning women must test you first to see if you are for real. While I tend to agree with such a theory, I don't believe they do it on a conscious level. More like women don't know how they feel about a stranger they just met. In such a short time, unless they are boozed up, they are unsure whether they should be kissing a stranger. Then you must take the lead; you must make the decision for them.

When you are running this type of hardcore closing game, you are going to have to make decisions for women all the time. Unless you take the initiative, girls won't go home with you. If you get into the habit of closing regardless of their reactions, you will end up with a lot of one night stands and more sexual partners than you can handle.

But if you don't, you will be left with lots of meaningless conversations in clubs that never led to sex. You will be frustrated.

Can You Close The Deal Without Getting Physical With Women?

Some folks think they can get laid using only Verbal Game. It's comparable to trying to grow muscle by only lifting light weights. You won't succeed at taking girls home. I have had some amazing students with million dollar mouthpieces, who would not get laid unless they added a strong physical component to interactions.

Many guys are just happy if they make girls giggle and talk back to them. It creates what I would like to call "an illusion of attraction." Most times, these guys are entertainers. They just make women have fun while they, themselves, have no fun at all. This is so typical in this game, because most guys are looking for validation from women out there. They are happy with just getting girls to approve of them, because it meets that need to be accepted by the opposite sex. But sooner rather than later, you will resent it. If night after night you go out to entertain and be liked by women, while not getting any tangible results, you will be disappointed and feel you have been short changed. Carrying water for people will do that to you.

Some men believe if women like them, they don't have to lead. They delude themselves into thinking if females laugh at their jokes, they don't have to do uncomfortable things that would challenge approval from the girls (for example, pulling them close to their bodies, and being sexual with them). However, if you don't lead, you will never get laid.

On the other hand, you cannot lead if you are afraid of what they think of you. To tip the scale, you must risk losing their approval – an uncomfortable prospect for a guy trying to woo the opposite sex. This compromising creed of being liked will have a crippling impact on your closing game. If you are unable to lead physically, you will find it next to impossible to get laid.

What's An Extraction?

You take your girl out of the club somewhere. As a Closer, you must turn into an extraction machine. Depending on where you are taking her, you have different types of extractions. For example, if you take her out for food, we call it "food extraction."

On this food extraction, you tell your girl at various times during the night you are planning on taking her to a great eating place later because you are usually hungry after clubbing. Then you keep repeating that throughout your night – you say things at various times like: "I am so hungry. I need to eat." Or: "This place serves the best pizza ever, I am taking you to check it out later." So when the club closes you have the perfect alibi to drag her out of the club with you.

Food extractions are simple to use because of their seemingly harmless nature. Girls play along to it with ease. However, don't be fooled. They know if they agree to walk out of the club with a guy, it means sex. For this particular reason, you are not obliged to take her for food but straight back to your place.

For example, jump in a cab with her and instruct the driver to take you home. Don't answer any enquiry from your girl about where you are going and respond: "It's ok, it is going to be fun" to any question. Keep talking to her all the time and assume she agreed to go home with you – your key to an extraction. Engage her by talking of something else while you drive her to your place. Believe me, she knows.

As it is by far the most difficult and challenging aspect, I love to coach this make or break last gasp of the game. Frustrating when you fail, but rewarding when you pull it off, towing a girl out of a club onto the street, and getting her to jump in a cab or walk home with you can be hard. Yet you cannot find anything more exhilarating or satisfying.

It will get ugly before it gets good. You will feel awkward at first – from pushing a girl's head on into a cab, police arrest style, to engaging in a tug of war with her friends at the end of the night. Consider this the last piece in the puzzle, which has all the makings for a drama or comedy script. In repeating this drama every night you go out you will become a master – a Dalai Lama of pulling.

You want to make your 2000 rookie mistakes fast so you can move on to your 2000 master mistakes. To succeed you must try to pull home every girl you meet –ABP – *Always Be Pulling*. No other rule of thumb for novices will yield more results faster: run the train on every girl and try to take her home.

Car Extraction

I used to have a problem when I went out of town to Pick Up girls. I didn't have a place to go back to for a one-night stand. Because the town where I used to live in Spain was kind of a small pond, which I over-fished in two years by picking up girls every weekend in the same three or four hot venues in town, I felt the need to expand my horizons onto the next population. Though it was cool to go to venues where nobody knew me, it was kind of a drag because I couldn't pull girls straight home. It was a one hour drive. So, instead, I decided to take them to my car and have sex there – hence car extractions. In car extractions, you follow the same routine as in food extractions. In fact, all extraction methods can be used.

Sometimes, I would tell a girl I would drive her home at the end of the night. I kept repeating that all night so when it was time to go home, she already knew what was happening. So I took her to my car – and you would not believe how fast clothes go off when you are alone. It was so effective, and I got so little resistance in my car, I decided it was even better than taking them home. My car was an old beat up Ford Fiesta, which was so small it resembled a box of matches with two doors. Still women had no problem having uncomfortable sex there.

Alternatively, you can tell your girl you want to go for a walk outside because you want some fresh air. Then once you are outside, you "randomly" walk to your car – then, act surprised when you come across it. Jump in and tell her that you want her to listen to your favourite band. Once she gets in there, escalate, kiss, – and clothes go off.

To achieve this extraction, I suggest parking your car in a sex friendly location, possibly a dark remote alley or parking lot. That way, you will have no interruptions during sex from people passing by. Sometimes morning daylight would find me in my car having sex with a girl while passers by shouted insults and jokes at me and my girl.

You would think this would put off women. Quite the contrary. Many girls I had sex with, were turned on by strangers watching and would say something along the lines of, "they are just jealous." It blew my mind that they were more comfortable than I was. They didn't give a damn what people thought of them.

The Simple "Let's Go" Extraction

The "Let's go" extraction, on the other hand, means not explaining yourself at all. Like the name says, it is just about leading. Grab her by the arm and say: "Let's go." She will ask "Where?" and you say: "Don't worry. It will be fun". And keep pulling her arm to go with you.

Don't get specific about your intentions and instead lead her firmly out of the club. Expect resistance and be ready to pull through it. Don't talk much and be curt in this type of pull. However, when you perform a stunt like this you need a lot of physical leading prior to it, for she needs to be in the habit of "following you around."

Are You Afraid Of Getting Into A Tug Of War With The Other Girls In The Group?

Unless you are leading physically, you will not be able to extract. Even when you are at your best at steering groups and girls, you won't be able to pull. Pulling girls from clubs home involves a great deal of trust on the part of the girl. She has to be psyched about you to leave the club with a guy she just met. Unless you take full command, it cannot be done.

Don't try to look good, but get it done. If necessary engage in a tug of war with the girls in the group: you pulling your girl on one side and the girls pulling your chick on the other. It is going to get messy if you want to have the sex life of your dreams. You need to let go of approval seeking and looking perfect all the time. Be ready for imperfection. Thrive on it. Adopt the mantra "if it is worth doing, it is worth doing it poorly." But get it done.

Failing costs nothing and teaches valuable lessons. Take erring as an indication you are applying yourself and pushing the limits of reality. I don't like it when guys don't get rejected in a night out with me. In shrinking from mistakes, you forever remain in comfort zone territory.

I keep saying to students, "Unless you lose lots of girls, you won't get lots of girls." It proves challenging because most guys are hard wired to acceptance. In reverting to that kind of mentality (thinking the more you lose the more you gain in the long run) lies the secret to becoming a closer. A closer swears by the abundance mentality of an unlimited supply of women, so why bother about losing one?

What Is A Good Trick for Pulling?

I used to bounce girls from a club to an after-hours joint where everybody knew me – a venue that was a hangout for the baseball team I used to play for. My team mates would go there every weekend with girlfriends, wives and relatives. Those same people came to all our baseball games. They were our whole fan base, if you will. When I showed up at the door at around three in the morning and everybody was a little boozed up already, it was like Elvis entered the building.

Guys and girls ran towards me and hugged me, high-fived me and offered me a drink – even the band that was playing would wave at me. It was some serious rock star treatment. I took every girl I pulled from clubs there prior to going home. When a girl saw this commotion in my presence, she would just fall head over heels for me. It was my end game. Now she wanted to have me. It worked every time, so I kept playing this trick over and over. Every weekend, I brought a different girl and the reaction was like clockwork.

I took women there and ignored them for a bit while I talked to my buddies. This type of disinterest got her so attracted to me that the next logical step was sex. Others did all the attraction work for me: she got approached by my buddies' girlfriends and asked if I was her boyfriend. This raised my value to her and helped to amplify attraction.

Then, all my buddies' girlfriends, good friends of mine, would proceed to "sell me" to her. It was beautiful. No work required. By the time we left the place later she just wanted sex with me. The validation I received from all my friends made her think I was the ideal candidate for sex. Though this approach may sound Darwinist, with women choosing the strongest candidate for sex, I must urge you not to look at it that way. There's nothing Darwinist about bringing her into your world. If anything, consider it an act of honesty.

Working A Group Of Two Girls

I have heard the same question a million times on program, on the road, and on workshops: how can you pull from a group of two girls? The rationale: you can't separate two girls who came together to the club.

My experience tells me these are the easiest groups to pull from. Experience also tells me one girl of the two wants a guy. Or, best case scenario, they are both looking. So if you work it smart, and do not make stupid mistakes, you might wind up with something.

Without ignoring either one, you must befriend them both the same way and proceed to give a little more attention to the one you like. This will prevent cock-block scenarios at the time of pulling.

> ### Reality Check
>
> *Rookies ignore the friend and focus only on the girl they like. This can have long term consequences down the road. If you befriend only one girl at the expense of the other, then the other one feels left out and will end up attempting to take your girl away from you. She fears her friend might go home with you and she will be left alone to fend for herself.*

You patch this dangerous dynamic by making sure the other girl gets your attention, thus reassuring her she won't be left alone. You want to engage her, compliment her, dance with her. You need to keep a neat balance of attention between your girl and her girlfriend.

What Happens Down The Line On A Two Set Scenario?

If your girl likes you and the other sees it, she will excuse herself to go to the toilet or to the bar for a drink. Think of this as your cue to amp things up, escalate physically and kiss close. She will give you a window of 10 to 20 minutes before she comes back. You better close your deal in that time frame.

When she comes back you need to resume treating her the same way – with lots of attention and care. Once you have made out in the window she gave you by going to the toilet/bar, you must spend the rest of the night with them, and make sure they both have a good time with you. I have done this routine countless times and arrived at the end of the night with the other girl as my ally in pulling by insisting we should go home together.

All the extraction techniques mentioned above can be used. At the end of the night, when the club closes and you have to go, you just have to stand back and watch how they discuss the logistics of what's going down.

Alternatively, towards the end of the night, I tell my girl to tell her friend we are going for food or something, depending on the type of extraction I am using. Then I sit back and watch them work it out. If you did your job right, and the other girl likes you, you have a high probability of pulling that night. Not only will she tell her friend she doesn't mind going home alone, but also encourage her to leave with you. She will become your ally. If, on the contrary, you sadly made the mistake of ignoring her, you will have a cock-block scenario in your hands.

Moreover, you can work the group of two for a threesome. In fact, I always work the group of two with the idea of pulling them both. I know most girls in groups of two in clubs are looking for sex in general. I try to make out with both of them and then try to pull them both out of the club. If you use those extraction techniques mentioned earlier and get good at them, you will end up in your apartment with two girls instead of one and with lots of threesomes under your belt.

Bring A Chode In!

As a safe variant, you can find the worst looking guy around and introduce him to the other girl. While he keeps her entertained, you can take your girl onto the dance floor or to the bar, or find a safe place to make out and get physical. I have done this several times and it always works.

It's a win/win. On the one hand you are giving a girl to a guy who doesn't have any skills. (Some guys are so grateful that they buy you drinks and suck up to you all night.) And on the other hand, the other girl wins too because she has somebody to talk to while you work on her friend. This scheme works every time on a group of two girls. Extraction becomes easier when the other girl doesn't feel she will be left stranded and alone for the rest of the night. Same extraction tactics mentioned above apply when you work with another guy in your group.

Cock-blockery And Group Leader Theory

Being successful at extractions – your key move to getting laid – has a direct relationship with how good you are at prevention of cock-blockery. Prevention has to do with early identification of common threats, for example, the ever-feared group leader. You will recognize her as the one pulling the strings of the group – so you need to spot her early.

From my experience, a group leader turns out to be a fatty, a midget, or an ugly girl, or a combination. Alternatively, you also get the occasional gay guy. Peer pressure or leader pressure will make a girl reject you even when she likes you. The group will do what these leaders say. The dominant girl in the flock decides whether a guy can hang out with them or even gives the green light for sleeping with any of the girls in her group – meet the go-to girl.

When you hang out with a group of girls make it a point to identify this matron-of-sorts early and get her on your side, because down the line you are going to need her. It has happened to me on several occasions. I do everything right, I approach the group, befriend them, pluck a girl, make out with her, bring her back, hang out for a long time to end up failing to pull, because the midget group boss decides they are going to another club which is "much more fun than this one."

Since the group chief whip has more pull than I do, my girl ends up dragged away by the ringmaster. Bummer: You spent the night with a girl, and you are left with a hard on and nothing but a phone number that might not even be solid... and a lesson to be learned. Life comes down to a few moments – so does a pull.

My group leader theory says you need to identify the go-to girl in the group early and befriend her if you are to pull a girl from her group.

My life in the field became easier when I started identifying key elements in the group and taking care of threats in a timely fashion. I became more efficient at pulling. That's why I instruct students to befriend everybody in the group as a priority – because I know somewhere inside the group, you will run into a group leader. Without the seal of approval of the main girl, guys have a harder time when extraction time comes. Like that famous quote from the sensational book, *The Art of War*, "A battle is won before it is ever fought."

Getting Laid Is What Happens To You When You Are Busy Having Fun

If you look at the times when you got laid, you will find one common denominator: fun.

Your girl was having fun, you were having fun, and, as a result, your dick finds its way into her pants. One thing led to another, everything seemed to fall into place and you went home together. It was almost meant to be. If you pay closer attention, you will notice that there was not much of an effort. It all flowed somehow. Although you have your usual bumps in the road, maybe a bit of resistance, you kissed the girl and got success because you were simply having fun.

I would go as far as saying that when you are not in a good mood or having fun, your chances of getting laid get reduced to zero. No fun: you can't start conversations. No fun: you can't maintain an interaction based on logical conversation. No fun: you can't drag her away from her friends anywhere.

The whole system breaks when the one obvious thing that glues it together breaks: fun— enjoyment, happiness, good mood, state, good vibe, and high energy.

If you go out to have a ball, the rest takes care of itself. Techniques, strategies and tactics will all fall into place with repetition – but having a good time goes further and deeper in the game. A master enjoys his practice first, and everything else is a by-product of his enjoyment.

CHAPTER 14

The Pitfalls

Discover Where the Hidden Landmines Are. And Some By-ways

This chapter is intended as a trouble-shooting guide for those who struggle. From years of experience I know the problems that afflict most guys when they start. I crawled my way out of these pitfalls myself and have the scars to show for it. Today, I teach them to students so they don't have to go through them – thus, shrinking their learning curve.

The Positive State Killers

Enthusiasm or positive state fuels your practice. Without it, you are lost. Nobody, especially no girl (unless she is a weirdo), wants to be around somebody with a negative attitude. I will detail the things that cause you to fall into negative states of mind.

By knowing where the common landmines are you will make sure you walk past them without stepping on them and blowing your mental state up. These pitfalls are typical of mistakes guys make in their practice. I have been collecting them over the years by careful observation of my students and myself. With time, I have been able to identify, classify and design strategies so that my clients don't have to suffer them.

In the same vein, not only I will teach you how to avoid them, but I will also explain how to create positive feelings and preserve them when you are in the thick of practicing your game.

Girl's Reactions vs Your State

Most guys depend on the outside world for positive feedback. We are hooked on it. Since we males are more outwards oriented, unlike females, we are always scouting the environment for signs of how we are doing or what we are supposed to do.

Males are movers and changers. We are programmed to alter the environment and look out for prey. We were hunters in prehistoric times: namely, an otherwise ok behaviour, which proves deadly in a club. Since we are outwards oriented, we look for feedback in the environment about how we are doing. So, if women accept us, laugh at our jokes or give us approval, we are doing fine. We feel on top. If, on the contrary, we get disapproval and rejection, we are doing wrong. We feel foul inside.

So, approaching women turns into a roller coaster of emotions. If they like you, you feel valuable. If they don't, you feel worthless. In other words, the more they like you, the more you like yourself. If they don't, you hate yourself. This is applicable to 99 percent of the guys out there.

The residual one percent, not validated from outside, is a rare breed. I have found some on my programs but they are the exception. Female approval is like candy; everybody wants some.

Which takes me to my next point.

Pressure To Be Liked

Due to the pressure to be liked in social settings, it feels like all eyes are on you and judging your actions all the time. The "people must like me" thought will cross your head once in a while – and at times it will be the sole thing in your mind. Trying to be liked creates an insurmountable amount of extra pressure when you start a conversation with a stranger. You feel like you failed them when they don't like you.

Nothing could be further from the truth.

If your state (good emotions, passion and enthusiasm for approaching women) depends on a female's validating reactions towards you, going out every night will be like walking the tight rope. You will find yourself swinging in your emotions and moods. It will short-circuit your practice.

You must practice not owning other people's feelings. You need to realise that people's feelings are theirs, not yours. You didn't cause them. You had nothing to do with them. If a girl is having a bad night in the club, she will lash out at anybody who approaches her. What makes you think she is going to act differently towards you? But she is the one having an awful night, not you. You cannot be responsible for her feelings and emotions.

Approval from inside must replace external validation. You need to approve of your actions by giving yourself full marks for approaching people. Give yourself nothing but praise for being social – though others might not think much of it. External regard (hollow approval) must not steer your ship in the turbulent waters of a packed club.

Approving Of Your Story

Even if you are talking about your day, and the ordinary events that happened to you up until you arrived at the club, you need to give thorough approval to your story. No matter what! Say: "I woke up this morning. I went to the airport. Bus was late. I grabbed a coffee when I arrived to the terminal. I jumped on the plane. I sat next to a funny looking guy. We talked football". If you judge your story to be boring (you don't approve of it), that's how people relate to it. I want you to approve of it and get excited about it. Because it comes from your unique perspective, it is your story. I want to challenge you to give approval to your worst and tell them to people.

> **COACH DRILL**
>
> Tell a 60 second story about your day. Give it approval. Believe in your heart that it is ok to talk to people about it because it happened during your day. Say that story to a minimum of 20 girls in one night. Don't look for approval when you do it. Some girls will like it, others won't. You need to be ok with all responses, good or bad. Start on the path of giving approval from inside to your own stories. Don't look for your environment to approve of things. If a girl interrupts you with questions, answer her questions and be prepared to go wherever the conversation takes you. For better results, you must not embellish your story with grandiose hyperboles or jokes. In other words, don't tell a "cool" story. Tell it like it is. Be ok with whatever feedback you get from random people. Some will find it interesting. Others won't. This exercise is going to challenge you in many ways. You won't get approval all the time and you must remind yourself you don't need it.

Self-Evaluation vs Your State

Self-evaluation (or self-measuring) happens when you compare yourself to somebody else's standard. Once this behaviour sets in, self-doubt is just a stone's throw away.

People tend to evaluate themselves against somebody else's standards. In other words, you measure your performance against somebody else's. I get this all the time on my program because students tend to compare themselves with other students in the program. If they perceive they are not measuring up to the progress of the next guy, they feel bad about themselves.

At other times, guys measure themselves against a standard of perfection they have in their heads. Unless they are performing to that standard, they get a severe blow to their motivation to practice the game. As their mental state shuts down, they turn inwards, into their head, straight into paralysis.

As males, we are pushed to compete in this society for power, status, and money. It isn't by chance that this dynamic appears on a

Pick Up program. Yet in succumbing to it, most guys damage their progress in the game. Everybody grows at his own pace. You cannot go faster than you are already going. Trying to go faster than you can go will be detrimental to your practice. You will force yourself to do things you are not ready to do yet. You may try hard, but you won't get what you want in the end.

Every next level of skill is built upon lesser levels. You must learn to walk before you can run. If you learn to run before you walk, you will walk funny. For that reason, you need to stop measuring yourself against other people.

First of all, you need to stop judging things as "good" or "bad". An either/or mentality is inexpedient to your own practice. It means you need to stop grading interactions into good or suck. Why? Because when guys evaluate interactions into good or bad they tend to use the good reaction measuring stick. If the reactions are good, their performance is good as well. If they get rejected, it is a bad performance.

Then, if they get a long streak of bad reactions, most guys feel depressed and stop approaching for fear of getting another bad rating. Alternatively, you can turn into an approval junkie because good reactions mean good game in your book.

The rating system ends up controlling your behaviour, not the opposite. You should be your master, not the slave of your measuring system.

The same applies to the all pervasive good/bad night syndrome. Once the night ends, on the way home, a guy rates the night into a good night or a bad night. His motivation and feelings of self worth will depend on how well he performed. As a result, because nights can go either way depending on the criteria for success followed, he will walk the tight rope every night. Motivation for going out will diminish over time – since talking to women becomes a performance test or an exam.

To eliminate this, monthly goals must be put in place and you must defer revising them until the end of the month. It means, during your month, that you don't do any measuring. That way you spare yourself the trouble of self-criticism for not performing up to par. I designated a section in this chapter for goal setting. Stay tuned for that.

Refusing To Do A Bad Job

You can destroy your endeavours to become a master by not being willing to make mistakes. Big, fat, gross ones. I am talking outright failure.

I tell my students: "I want you to fail." That's right. I am supposed to teach "Success with Women", but instead I end up teaching guys how to fall. But I didn't invent this. When I first started learning judo (I wanted to defend myself against my primary school bullies, of course, what's a scrawny kid to do?), my judo teacher taught me how to fall for my first two weeks. For two long weeks, I was not taught anything at all except how to break a fall. He made me land on my back for hours on end. It was the single most boring, uncomfortable thing I have ever done, but it taught me a great principle of mastery: learn to break a fall. I apply this principle with diligence to Pick Up. I teach guys how to fall.

"If it is worth doing, it is worth doing it poorly," I say all the time. I chant: "I don't care how you do it, just get it done." Get a girl mad at you because you tried to steal her away from her group. Get a feeling of what it means to fail and you will lose your respect for failure. At some point, it should not count as failure but as a natural progression to your goal. I want to see you pulling a girl by the hand to the dance floor and your girl pulling the other way, visibly uncomfortable and trying to get away from you. Believe me, struggling with girls is the stuff make outs are made of.

Reality Check

Make a mess as prerequisite to gaining a skill. I tell my beginner students: "I want you to make your 2000 rookie mistakes as soon as possible." That way they move on to what I call the master's mistakes. In other words, what people call "quality problems" – like a rich man deciding which million dollar house to buy.

The Hollywood Movie

Some people approach their nights like a Hollywood action movie. It starts good, gets great, and finally ends awesome. Fiction stories, especially Hollywood, run the same plot in every movie they make. They have educated the public on it so much through the years that we expect the same thing when we go to the cinema: good, then great, and awesome at the end. However, the reality of Pick Up doesn't run according to a script.

You might go out at 10pm, start approaching and suck for a while; then, around midnight, you might start a conversation with some amazing girl who likes you but has to go back to her friends and leaves you alone – which makes you irritable because you are left with a phone number instead of a girl. After that, it all goes downhill until the end – with no promising interactions. On other nights, however, you feel on top of the world and everything you touch turns into gold. You have many make outs, connect with girls at a deeper emotional level and you take a girl home.

With a lack of a rigid script (you might suck on Friday, go amazing on Saturday and crash and burn all Sunday or the other way around), every night unfolds like an adventure. It's the unpredictable sine qua non of this game. Instead of a boring cinematic experience, go out to live a new experience. Don't expect the same boring Hollywood fairy tale every night you hit the club.

Frustration always comes from unfulfilled expectations, especially impossible ones. Have realistic expectations and you won't be disappointed.

Instinct vs. Logic

The spin stops here. No more spinning of logic. Once you step into a club all reasoning must go out the window. Rationalism kills the fun – thus preventing you from getting laid. People love to dissect the game into meaningful parts. Stop being rational. You must remove "Why?", "When?", "How?" from your vocabulary. These are all questions with a background of logic behind them. You need to stop that type of questioning. It prevents you from having a ball.

The Physical Game

Make a commitment to stop logic when you are in the field. Make a deal with your wing to give him 10 dollars every time you start a rational conversation. Either you will make your wing rich or you will be forced to have fun.

You can apply this little pay off scheme to being negative too. Pay off your wing when you make a negative comment. Pay your wing 10 bucks every time you see a hot girl and you don't approach. Etc.

> *Reality Check*
>
> *When in the field, don't pick your groups. Approach the first one you see. Instead of scanning the room for the hot and easy group of girls to approach, move and start a conversation with the nearest group of girls to you. I make a habit out of approaching the first girl(s) I see on my programs. For example: I give my final instructions for the night to my students in a huddle, I turn around and I approach the first adjacent group of people, no matter what. This allows me to jump into the action straight away, disengaging the powerful logical side of my brain by not giving it time to engage. If you allow logical thinking to set in by analysing, scanning and figuring out the environment, you will be at a disadvantage when you start approaching. Get your first group out of the way fast by jumping into the middle of the action without delay.*

Zero Logic Point In The Club

It occurs when your actions are rooted in instinct, not in calculation – otherwise called "flow." It coincides with that time when you are having the most fun. Some call it "state" – (not to be confused with a high.) You are not necessarily jumping up and down like a maniac, but your logical side does not govern you. Instead, everything flows without inner resistance. You don't make a strong effort when you approach, but you seem to get it done without trying.

Zero logic point causes you to talk without asking a lot of questions (otherwise known as interview style –you know, the typical drone of lame guys in night clubs: "What's your name?", "Where are you from?"

etc.) All questions disappear while in the flow and you want to share with people who you are. When you reach this illogical point in the night you will see your conversation going into unexpected topics – fruits you like, types of salad dressings, your best sex ever, etc. Girls get into it because you are no longer a slave to the conventions of typical conversations.

This happens when you drop all logic and go with your gut.

Looking At Women as Targets and Groups of People as Sets

In most Pick Up circles, guys look at girls as game, as 'targets': an object to be obtained, or a cherished possession. They also refer to groups of people as 'sets'." The word 'set' comes from show business, where you are supposed to perform in front of an audience for a certain amount of time, which they call a 'set'. You need to understand that having this kind of mentality will make you appear weird when you talk to people.

For starters, women are not targets or objects to be acquired, but people like you and me. On the other hand, they are not sets because you are not doing a show. You just walk up to them to be social and find out whether you like her or not – instead of entertaining or performing to them.

I have seen many guys spoiled with the above game mentality. Looking at women as targets or objects to be conquered will make you needy in the field. You will fail to connect with them at a more human level. You will be deemed weird. Plus women, will resent being seen as a target or an object rather than a human being. Other words that come to mind to describe this behaviour are "unnatural," "scripted," "approval seeking". Furthermore, seeing women as "cherished, valuable possessions" will put them right above you, on a pedestal and so make them very uncomfortable to relate to.

You must shed this game mentality and become normal and natural around people. People will react in kind. Real growth cannot be faked; you must pay your price. You must try and err until you are able to be comfortable being yourself around groups and beautiful women. It will take time before you can see females as equals – not above, not below you. Your creed must be patience.

Negative Filtering. Focusing On Mistakes

Guys have a tendency to try to fix what's wrong. We are fixer uppers. Some are obsessed about improving those things they think they lack or need fixing – at the expense of ignoring their very own unique qualities. Nothing wrong with self-actualizing yourself but in the process you don't want to kill the goose that lays the golden eggs, a.k.a., YOU.

By focusing on mistakes and things you lack, you make them grow bigger. The problem is the way we see the problem. If you see yourself as a defective item, other people will look at you like that too. You will not be so confident because by "fixing" yourself all the time, you reinforce the idea you are skewed.

When you only filter what's wrong about you, you create a self-image of low quality. This less-than-ideal image will be somehow projected on to others when you speak to them. You will be communicating exactly the opposite of what you want.

I challenge you to filter the positive about you. If you are a fixer upper the next exercise will be a trying one.

> ### COACH DRILL
>
> Take a piece of paper and draw two columns. In one, write all the things you consider your good qualities and, on the other, your bad qualities. If your bad qualities far exceed the good qualities you are a victim of this defective item syndrome. You probably spend too much time trying to fix yourself because you look at yourself as defective, faulty, etc. You will encounter a lot of resistance submitting yourself to the practice of Pick Up, a discipline that requires tons of flexibility and ample room for error. You probably are a "fixer upper," somebody who focuses on problems and defects rather than strengths. Too much time in the dark and very little in the light. You will remain forever in darkness.
>
> Try and increase the list of good qualities about yourself every day. Instead of noticing your shortcomings start to spot your good qualities. Expand your positive traits list until it grows bigger and better than the negative traits. After that, blow your positive out of proportion. Focus on it, tell the girls about it:
>
> "I love having fun. Fun is my number one quality. Are you any fun?" I have started conversations with that line for years. I have grown comfortable talking about my positive qualities without bragging—in a normal manner. You have been doing the opposite. Time to change and do something that benefits you.

The Big Picture In Pick Up

In the process of learning, you need to embrace the little positive things. Most people balloon the bad out of proportion and minimize the positive. Your Average Joe leaves the club and only remembers the girl that rejected him and, somehow, forgets the other dozen girls who did talk to him and found him enjoyable and interesting company. In this respect I must go with George Leonard's advice in his excellent book, *Mastery*: "accentuate the positive and acknowledge the negative." And not the other way around.

You must distil your positive aspects out of every interaction and acknowledge your negative without focusing on it. This will keep you in a right frame of mind to learn. I want you to get to the point that you can leave the club after four hours of solid approaching and only remember the good things. There was some negative – but your mind has been trained through repetition not to give it a whole lot of thought. Eventually, you will become what I like to call delusionally positive.

This way, negative things like rejection will lose their hold on you. Your brain will stop looking to fix and you will be able to focus on learning. Having a defective mentality or fixer upper orientation will make you too outcome dependent – therefore ruining your practice and causing you to lose motivation to go out. You need to look at the big picture. Losing one battle – one girl – doesn't mean you have lost the war. You must consider this a marathon – and one where you will get everything right over time if you keep running.

Fighting A Bad Mental State

Most guys tend to fight back their mental state by pretending bad feelings are not there. They stuff their bad feelings down so much that they create a huge amount of mental pressure. As a result, they render themselves incapable of approaching, because they don't feel comfortable with those foul feelings bottled up. You need to imagine a champagne bottle ready to bust open with a little cork on it that cannot hold the bursting bubbles in. That's how guys feel when they fight their feelings of inadequacy in the club.

I go by one mantra on my program: "acknowledge feelings and take appropriate action." Say to yourself that you are afraid, but that you will do it anyway. Don't let the fear stop you. Don't try to make it go away either. If you spot it and you act according to the situation, fear will lose its paralysing grip. With no real danger but fear of rejection, you will find once threatening situations ordinary to say the least. As soon as you realize (by approaching) that people are not out to reject you as you thought, your fear will lose its hold and your approaching will be kicked into gear.

I have another successful mantra I use all the time. It goes by the acronym of DIWA (do it while afraid).

A lot of time is wasted thinking about how to destroy fear, and overcome approach anxiety, as if fear is the enemy. But haven't you done anything while afraid? Have you ever jumped in a pool while thinking the water will be cold?

If you think long and hard you will find you have done many things in your life while afraid. Not only that, you accomplished your ultimate goal, scared. I played baseball for eight plus years, and though I like the game, there were moments when I was fearful. Yet, I managed to get it done. Off the top of my head, I remember home games with a bit of a crowd and me struggling to get a starting job in the line-up against much better peer players. (Some were in professional leagues and I was just a weekend warrior.) I went out one time and hit two for three on a home game against a tough opposing pitcher – I put on quite a performance that day. I got props from everybody including the coach. I did it all afraid. Since there was more pressure inside the team for starting jobs, I was always proving my worth to the team. Notice how I didn't pretend my fear was not there. Nor did I bottle it up. I dealt with it effectively. I *DIWA-ed.*

Discipline means doing something that is not fun to do. You might not fancy ploughing through rejection in a club – though with time you might find it amusing. However, the fear of such pain, not the pain itself, prevents you from making progress.

Progress means pressing through the pain of rejection, confronting and acknowledging it. To stand in front of a girl, trying to talk to her, reacting to her anger, you will feel a fear eating at you, the first time around. As you press on rather than run away and hide, you will look fear in the eye, causing you to lose respect for it. Your pain in itself could never match your fear of it. It can be compared to bullies that turn out to be less scary once you get to know them, and you see that they are just real people with an attitude.

"I Don't Like To Go On Stage Unless I Have Butterflies In My Stomach." Or Something

I can't remember the exact quote from Elvis Presley. But he admitted his fear when he was to face an audience. He deemed it necessary to feel anxiety prior to a performance in order to do it right. Here is a guy who made a habit of doing it afraid. He knew he was fallible. Too bad he was a self destructive individual – but the lesson remains. He knew he was afraid but didn't panic.

I have made a lifestyle out of doing it afraid. I have talked to audiences larger than I thought I could. I have opened groups I knew were going to be tougher for me than I could handle. I have run programs in conditions that I thought were impossible. You would think by this time I wouldn't be afraid. Nope. I am still afraid. I suspect I will be for as long as I live. It's part of life.

I asked a scared student once to approach girls with: "I am lost. I don't know what I am doing here. Can you help me?" Because of his sincerity, many girls in the club wanted to talk to him and find out more about him. Now, if I had forced upon him some cocky opener and some tough-it-up attitude, he would no doubt have crashed and burned. It would have been pretending, and the girls would have seen right through him. Rather than glorifying fear, I just don't want you to make a big deal out of it. Instead, like Elvis, use it to your advantage.

Watching vs. Doing. The Spectator Mode

Many fall into this trap. It happens after a couple of rejections or at the beginning of the night when guys decide to be idle and postpone any action until later. Of course, they find it easier not to approach women and stand by and watch. Some rationalize it by saying: "I am going to watch social interactions and learn." Or: "I will wait until the club is full to start approaching." There are many ways to justify being in your comfort zone. I just mentioned some of the most common.

When you fall into passivity like this, you must spot yourself first. You need to understand why you are falling into spectator mode and not taking action. Either you find it hard to start approaching (think of going to the gym and talking to your friends and delaying hitting the weights, because you don't feel like it), or you have had a couple of bad approaches where you were rejected and you feel like taking a break. These breaks prove costly. Not only will you sink further into non-action but you will also allow yourself to get logical about it. In other words, you run the risk of getting into your head and not acting by instinct like I have suggested you should before.

You can remedy this situation with swift action by approaching the group of people right next to you. Don't delay, take immediate action and disregard the result of your approach. You are doing this to break your inertia and build some momentum. You are doing it for you.

Even with a male group, converse for a while, get yourself out of your head and advance to other juicier groups with girls in them. But, first of all, break your spectator pattern by taking matters in your own hands. You will find yourself in spectator mode several times in the night. Consider it part of your job to spot yourself and interrupt this pattern. If you choose to stay idle, you will sink to the bottom and you will hate yourself for it. Your quick relief of not approaching and being inactive for a while will turn into long term self-loathing for not performing according to your expectations.

Vanity

Like Kevin Costner, playing the role of a minor league veteran catcher, told the young ace pitcher in the baseball movie *Durham Bulls*: "I know he is your father, but it doesn't mean he is not full of shit too." In the film, the ace pitcher was trying to pitch to impress his father, who was watching the game from the stands; but he was blowing it by trying to put on a good show. His delivery was whack because he wasn't focused on his pitching, but on impressing others.

Vanity is trying to impress your neighbour. And by neighbour, I mean friends, peers (other Pick Up guys), or your social circle. If you get an ego boost from picking up a girl before a crowd you are in deep trouble. Not only will you depend on them for feedback (negative for the most part), they will end up controlling your behaviour.

Under the pressure to perform for them, you will put extra weight on your shoulders to carry – and you will destroy your practice. You will not be practicing, you will be performing. You will eliminate the trial/error part of Pick Up because you don't want to disappoint your audience. Your internal self-worth will depend on how these groups rate you. Those groups will rate you down, never up, regardless and are never supportive (apart from a few exceptions that confirm the rule).

Furthermore, being vane and looking for recognition will not yield what you are looking for. I tell my students I am going to train them to be effective not to impress others.

It's not the Olympics. Nobody will give you a medal for taking a girl home. Chances are nobody will know about it. If you are taking this Pick Up training to heart, you will be going out three to four nights a week and most of your lays will be something between you and your girl. Nobody will pat you on your back and give you an "attaboy" for having sex with a girl at 3am in the morning. Same thing next day when you wake up next to her.

This game is meant to be played without much attention – unless you are a program instructor and you are demonstrating how to approach to students. I want my students to shed the external validation from their system as fast as they can. That's why I don't allow anybody to get away without some rejection on my program. They need to know how it feels to bite the dust many times. You need to grow immune to impressing others.

Playing To Win The Game in One Night

By playing to win, you play to lose. Being social and talking to people cannot be considered either a competition or a sport. Yet, guys go out with the same mindset of those who try to win a ball game. If you think this is a game, then women are your opponents. Outcome dependence will set in and you will bring upon yourself tremendous amounts of performance anxiety. While I played baseball, it was easy to crash the ball during batting practice, but it was ten times more difficult to face a real pitcher from the opposing team, who was trying to get you out – a real cat and mouse game. Obviously, we performed better on batting practice than in a real life game.

If you want to play such a cat and mouse game with girls, be my guest. Night venues are filled with the cadavers of players who have tried and failed. There is no need to bring in all the pressure and outcome dependence of a sport. This activity is about talking to people, befriending them, leading girls physically. If you apply a sport's hardcore mental approach towards outcome, you will only succeed at getting people defensive. Others might wonder why you are not having fun on a Friday night, and running around all serious with a "game face" on.

Remove your desire for an outcome from your activity and you will be golden. Becoming a victim of outcome dependence can hurt: when I turn to a student and command: "Approach the group behind you," his face turns to stone – as if he has been asked to take a Peñalty at the Soccer World Cup Final. Of course, his approach bombs.

For your average student, an approach is a test he has to pass to feel worthy. Pick Up is like a sport where he needs to win that night to feel good about himself. The way students approach the problem becomes the problem: self-worth increased with a good performance. It's ego based.

It took me some time to figure out my students needed to win this. It also rang true when I started to learn the game a long time ago. I used to go out and I didn't feel good unless I pulled a girl home at the end of the night. I became a one-night stand player. I needed the immediate results to feel good and worthy.

Unfortunately, this is contrary to the principles of mastery. No activity can provide a constant string of wins. Even the best players in any sport go through unproductive periods during a given season. The best remain calm and make it through the tough times. Unlike in a sport, you don't have to win every time.

Males are oriented to win. This society brainwashes guys into thinking either they are winners or losers. However, with no middle ground, bringing this ultra competitive mentality into human relations can cause problems. My solution has always been the same: temporary removal of outcome.

For example, at the beginning of the night, when I know guys are at the height of their performance anxiety, I instruct: "Let's make friends for 20 minutes. NO PICK UP!" It seems to work wonders. With no seduction related outcome in their heads, guys proceed to do some of their best performances of the night– namely, long interactions, make outs, impressive physical escalation. Look and see how I removed the outcome relating to Pick Up and gave them another outcome: to make friends. An alternative non Pick Up outcome will prevent you from struggling with having no goal. Males need goals – for they won't operate long without direction.

> ## COACH DRILL
> **Remove Outcome From Your Interaction**
>
> Approach a group of girls with the sole intention of making them laugh. Try not to use lame jokes to get a quick laugh. Once you have accomplished your laugh, you can pat yourself on the back and continue your interaction feeling good about yourself. Feel good because you made their night better. I use this drill with guys I call Obssessives. These guys need quick tangible results or they lose motivation. So by starting small, I keep them motivated and do not allow negative or perfectionist thoughts to come in. I make them climb the ladder to more challenging goals such as: "Now, go in and get physical in under five minutes." And then: "Now, pull her onto the dance floor as soon as you can." I increase the Pick Up relatedness of the outcome as I see the guy getting more and more confident and less obsessive about getting a result.

From Chode to Champ and Back To Chode

Nights where you feel awful will abound. Nights when not only you are not making any progress, but you are back to square one. In overcoming these nights lies real growth. You will not be made whole unless you go through some serious backsliding. Just as the smoker falls back into the habit, you will stumble into old patterns of behaviour because they feel more comfortable to you. Remember you had years to build your old behaviours, as opposed to the short time you've been with your new ones. So new behaviours will encounter lots of resistance in you. For example, you might find yourself by the bar unwilling or unable to approach.

Somehow you start to think that if you approach one more girl you will be sent to hell or they won't like you anyway so, why try? This garbage (otherwise called victim thinking) cannot be tolerated. We call this "chatter" in our trade as opposed to real analysis. It's best done outside the club.

Instead of fighting your inner resistance to forward motion, you will benefit by taking a step back. At this point, don't try to push through because you will fail and be frustrated in no time. If you expect to be rejected by the next girl, that's exactly what will happen – a self-fulfilling prophecy in action.

Take one step back and stop thinking of Pick Up or making girls like you. You need to unplug your Pick Up switch. It behoves you to start approaching – but instead, of seducing, make friends for a while. I use this simple technique of taking a step back from outcome (not to be confused with inaction) to get my students out of their heads and into the game at times when they are struggling in the field. Once they relax and have befriended enough people, and feel loose again, I get them back to doing whatever they were doing before: pulling girls to the dance floor, going for the make out, etc.

Somehow you have to cheat your head into doing something it doesn't want to do. You will not trigger too much inner resistance if you tell yourself you are just being social and take seduction out of the equation. I have been much criticized for taking Pick Up out of it by many guys who claim they are out to get women not to socialize. Though I respect their opinion, I must go with the path that offers minimum resistance to my students. I have found through practical experience that going out to be social makes it easier for guys to perform. In my experience the predatory attitude of going out to get sex creates a horny and needy vibe in most males that not only spooks the opposite sex, but also creates outcome dependence.

The same trick can be applied when we don't feel like going out and stay home and watch TV. We don't want to move out of the comfort of our own living room into the battle field of rejection – the club. But be that as it may, large numbers of girls gather there under one roof. Somehow you must trick your head into thinking that going to a club is much more fun than watching TV. Then you can also take a step and say to yourself: "I am just going to show up at the venue and make some friends and go home." Somehow your result or outcome (picking up women) must be taken out of the equation to make it easier to resolve your own inner resistance.

Most guys who get involved in Pick Up come from so-called nerdy backgrounds. They are accountants, IT men, or do computer related jobs or activities where they spend eight plus hours a day in front of a screen. Since they don't have the habit of being social they encounter resistance to going out and meeting new people. Because their jobs don't require people skills, they spend most of their time in their heads trying to figure out solutions to logical problems. However, approaching women has no logic to it. To beat their comfort zone mentality, they must find a way to stop Pick Up being a scary, rejection-filled activity.

The Mind Set Of "Not Now"

"Not now" proves to be by far the most fatal mindset in the field. Choosing "Not now" as your mantra means staying in the comfort zone, not embracing the unknown. One must acknowledge there won't be a perfect time to approach a girl, go for the kiss or start a conversation. You must get into the habit of not caring about the outcome of an interaction, and perform when circumstances don't seem to be ideal. Speed of execution is key and there should be total disregard for the result of your actions. Girls might choose not to talk to you and that's their prerogative. Your job is to execute.

My escalator drill works so well with all my students because, by executing approach after approach, they realize how futile overanalysing a situation can be. I make them approach girls in the worst of circumstances: moving up with the escalator, walking next to her, on an escalator going down and the girl going up, lots of people around. Moreover, they only have two minutes to talk to the girl because, at the end of the escalator, they must come back to me, lose their girl and start a new approach.

I make them walk up to girls like this over and over until I see they are enjoying the exercise of losing girl after girl. It feeds their brain with the idea that it is ok to do it now— though they are approaching in a less-than-perfect scenario.

It is better not to do it right than not at all.

Despite the imperfection of it all, most guys end up with phone numbers and mini dates out of that two-minute escalator jog. As soon as they start enjoying it, some girls will stop at the end of the escalator to talk to them. A guy who is amusing himself for real has never approached them.

Why You Won't Go Out Solo (Wing Man Dependence)

Ranking high as one of the biggest excuses not to go out, guys dread being in a club and asked the question: "Where are your friends?" and winding up looking like lonely weirdoes with no social circle.

Guys who need a wingman – or another guy to go out with – use his absence as an excuse to stay home. If you get in the habit of approaching with a wingman you will refuse to go out alone. You deem it tougher to approach alone, and ten times more difficult to pull a girl home without some help.

Well, I am here to tell you, "Guys who fly solo develop the tightest of games". They don't need people to back them up. They develop a strong resilience in the game– and one more thing, the dreadful question, "where are your friends?" never gets asked after a while. You will have to endure that question when you first start going out once in a while, to which you can respond with "I am lonely. I need a friend. Would you be my friend?" with a smirk in your face. Problem solved. Girls will giggle and never ask again. After some time and progressive improvement in the game, this uncomfortable question will not be asked, because women will be too busy trying to get to know you.

If you have a friend to go out with, fine. If not, go out alone and bite the bullet for a while and you will never look back. Enjoy the freedom of not depending on anybody. You are a one-man show.

"I Am Going To Get Laid Tonight."
Proper Goal Setting In Pick Up

Most guys don't know how to set up goals in this game. If you don't excel at writing your goals, you are planning failure. Most people phrase goals in terms of things not under their control, which can mean failure to convert. For example, "I will get laid tonight" doesn't depend entirely on you because the girls have a say in it. Since you cannot control other people's actions, you step into quick sand. Regardless of your good intentions, there is an X in the equation that cannot be filled by you. The girl has to approve of going home with you.

So, how do we phrase goals such that things we cannot control don't cripple us? Simply phrase your goals in terms of things you can influence. For instance, "On Friday, I am going to attempt to kiss close three girls." In order to accomplish that goal, you must make three kiss close attempts. Let's say you didn't get a single make out on Friday; then, reset the goal for Saturday and ditto for Sunday, etc.

How long? Well, until you get at least a make out.

A goal is written in concrete, but plans are made in sand. You might change the venue, the approach for the night, your clothes, or approaching girls with more verbal game, but the goal remains the same.

I guarantee if you attempt to kiss three girls or more every night that you are going to end up with something. That something doesn't concern me. But I only care about going for it – the attempt. *THAT* I can control and influence.

That's why most guys get bummed out at the end of the night because they focus their efforts on outcomes they cannot govern, like other people's reactions and behaviours. By bringing your attention and acting on things you can moderate, you are always winning. You are always ahead of the curve.

Most sluggers in professional baseball say homeruns happen. They say that because they know the outcome any time you step up to the plate cannot be guaranteed. There are too many variables outside their control. They can only focus on hitting the ball hard, or putting a great swing on the ball or getting a good pitch to hit. Homeruns occur when and with the concurrence of certain variables under the hitter's dominion such as: you put a great swing on the ball you get, you pick the right pitch to hit, you adjust to the pitcher's timing. Professional athletes choose to invest their efforts in those things within their area of influence. So should you.

Instead of saying, "I am going to get laid tonight," tell your friends or wingman, "I am going to attempt to pull a girl tonight." You feel empowered by a deed within your circle of influence: you can approach a girl and try to get her out of the club. If it doesn't happen that night, make it a point to try again the next night and so on until you get the job done. However, you choose to focus on elements of the game you can influence and control, namely, your behaviours and actions.

By the same token, goals should be established not for the one night, but for the long term. For example, you should have a set of goals for the weekend. Let's say you have a weekly goal of: "I am going to make-out with two girls this weekend." You phrase it in a proper manner and calculate how many girls you might need to attempt to approach to get it done. Let's say we go by the 80-20 rule, where, in 100 attempts you will get 20 results. You need to approach and attempt to kiss close 10 girls.

Then, you rephrase your goal in terms of things you can control: "I will attempt to kiss 10 girls this weekend. Five each day." Only revise your goals at the end of the weekend and do not try to assess yourself during the time you are in the club, because of the chance that you might kiss two girls in your last two attempts. The same criteria must be applied to monthly or longer term goals. You must defer evaluation until deadline or you risk losing your motivation.

By not evaluating yourself too soon, you avoid losing motivation and positive state – your power supply in the game. If you don't get your goals you reset the goal for the next month and so on. Never give up on your goals. The tide will turn for you when you least expect it.

Once you decide on a plan of action you must execute it without worrying whether it works or not. Postpone evaluation until later on, when you are done. Discipline yourself to withhold revision and gratification until you complete your task – despite your mind's pervasive habits of evaluating, assessing and "improving" your performance. Fight your wits with fists and teeth on this one and you will not be disappointed. Remind yourself your mind must be your servant, not your master.

I spend an average of one hour per program sitting down with the guys and teaching them how to set goals so that they are not frustrated in the field. Progress in the game can be traced back to proper goal planning, the key to success. With no planning, you are planning failure.

Epilogue

I hope this book was useful to you as a guide. I set out to write a practical book, the type of book that I wish I had when I started learning this game and was hitting my head against the wall more often than not.

In retrospect, all it takes is the right action and the development of new mindsets. I took lots of wrong actions and followed theories that looked like quick fixes, but couldn't stand the test of time. Independently of the type of theory you follow today, I am sure this book will be of help or complement you in some way.

If you are a rookie, looking for shortcuts is detrimental to your practice. Believing you can achieve any real growth without paying a price will delay your learning rather than favouring it.

About the Author

OSVALDO (A.K.A OZZIE) PEÑA GARCIA
Contact at:
www.pickupmadesimple.com
www.physicalgameblog.com
www.physicalgamebook.com
ozzie@realsocialdynamics.com

As an Executive Coach for all of Europe, Ozzie is based in London. Since 2005 he has worked for RSD-Real Social Dynamics-, the world's largest dating company with dating coaches based in Los Angeles, New York, London, Sydney, and San Francisco; programs are conducted in major metropolitan cities throughout North America, South America, Eastern/Western Europe, The Middle East, Asia and Australia.

After travelling around the world numerous times, Real Social Dynamics built dating coach mastermind groups. Executive Management hires dating coaches who are able to demonstrate their skills in the field, while teaching others; and each instructor have developed their own unique method to share with clients.

He was the second speaker in a successful DVD program teaching success with women called "Transformations".

Personally, he has been running live infield programs for approaching and bedding women since 2005. He joined RSD company-Real Social Dynamics- in 2004 and after gruelling training program for coaching men how to be successful with women, he started teaching pick up around the world. He travelled extensively around the globe teaching programs in all continents except Africa including the Middle East. He has run successfully programs in all major cities in the world and Europe.

His expertise in the field is cutting edge in the pickup industry.

He lives in London.

About Real Social Dynamics

www.realsocialdynamics.com

www.rsdnation.com

1(888)546-7286

Real Social Dynamics (RSD) is the world's largest dating coaching company. With dating coaches based in Los Angeles, New York, London, Sydney, and San Francisco, programs are conducted in major metropolitan English-speaking cities throughout North America, Europe, and Australia.

Through its LIVE world tours, Real Social Dynamics conducts Bootcamps and Superconferences, that have trained thousands of clients, including a diverse variety of individuals ranging from Fortune 100 executives, royalty, celebrities, college students, and professionals from over 70 different countries.

RSD specializes in dating advice, image consultation, public representation, and integrating clients into social scenes. Initially, live programs were offered solely through word of mouth via private clients. However, now, top-tier dating coaching is made available for the public via the Internet and direct phone contact with the RSD Headquarters in Los Angeles. RSD's dating coaching branch is a top-tier operation, run by the firm's best instructors, who invested thousands of hours of field research over the years meeting attractive women, and interviewing the world's most popular dating book authors, image consultants, and executive coaches.

RSD's dating coaching branch is a top-tier operation, run by the firm's best instructors, who invested thousands of hours of field research over the years meeting attractive women, and interviewing the world's most popular dating book authors, image consultants, and executive coaches.

RSD's Live Programs provide clients a unique opportunity to meet its dating coaches, become their wingmen, learn from countless hours of field research, witness dating coaches attract beautiful women in live demonstrations in real-world scenarios, and have them as their personal coach & image consultant.

RSD BOOTCAMP: An astonishing 3-day "mega-intense" live-in-field training program that obliterates all obstacles thwarting your success with women, the RSD Bootcamp has been meticulously honed since 2002 to guarantee nothing but undeniable, hard-hitting and instantly noticeable results.

Taught by some of the most extraordinary men on the planet...each executive coach is "hand-picked" personally by Executive Producer and RSD Co-Founder Owen Cook(aka "Tyler Durden") from amongst thousands of the world's most successful and qualified men who've applied.

With hyper-strict student/instructor ration of 3 to 1, nothing can compare to the riveting rush of challenging yourself to the core... blasting through success barriers and likely getting what most men would consider "lucky." We promise you will sharpen your pick-up skills to a razor's edge and instil a breakthrough "sexually abundant" paradigm in your reality or your money back...with our full "iron clad" 100% money back guarantee.

When you have mustered up the guts to man up and finally take immediate control of your love life, know that your Executive Coach is patiently waiting to launch you on the "fast track" to your new(and deserved) lifestyle of sexual abundance and dating success.

Absolutely open to all skill levels (as this program is tailored to you personally) and guaranteed, no matter who you are, to change your life forever.

http://www.realsocialdynamics.com/bootcamps.asp

Bootcamp Testimonials...

"I get tapped on the shoulder; Ozzie points to a girl nearby.I turn over to Alex for one second and right back around. Ozzie isnow making out with the girl that he pointed to.And not only that, he is almost thrown over by the girl kissing him,she is leaning in so hard .This is, I swear, no more than 3 sec. into the set. I was amazed!Hard to believe, well get a load of this:Me and Ozzie open a group of 4 girls plus boyfriend.Within minutes, not only is he grinding that guy's girl with himsmiling and just sitting there. We also get all four of the girlsplus a couple adjacent girls in a huge humping line, and have them grind away :)That's a big set for you.Never have I witnessed smoothness like that."

-Andy, London

"That night we again went sarging (picking up girls) to some clubs in the 'Puerto Olímpico', close to the beach of Barcelona. Ozzie gave me instructions on how to extract my target and take her to the beach and I only was thinking 'yeah, right', I never thought that I would get to that point. I started opening sets, using all the stuff Ozzie had showed me (how do you push a cow? With ALL you have!), doing kino (getting physical) right from the start. The first set went ok, the second set was great. I could not believe it, I was standing in set, doing lots of kino, hugging my target and she loved it! I played and teased and did all the kino stuff I had learned. I isolated my target and about 20 minutes in the set I took her to the dance floor and went for the kiss-close. It was my first game-related k-close and I did it after only 20 minutes in the set. I was on fire. The obstacle got mad, ran away and spent the rest of the night sending angry SMSs to my target, but she didn't give a and just was happy to hang out with me. I took her to the beach and we spent hours making out.

...the practice I gained sarging (picking up girls) with Ozzie pushed my game ahead big time: I got the balls to escalate, got a 'closer' mentality and I know that these field experiences will help me to calibrate my game. Thanx Ozzie, I really had a great time!"

-Fede, Barcelona.

"Ozzie,You said to let you know about success stories so here goes:We had a function on for my work and this guy bought with him a total 10. As she walked on the boat all the guys stared, all the the girls got jealous and I introduced myself. After getting plenty of attraction, I walked away with her number and talked to everyone else. I was controlling all the frames I was in and I knew she was sensing it (ie: that I was the coolest guy in the room) .Soon I went back in blew out the guys (I am sure you can see me doing this right now!), grabbed her hand and sat her down in a quiet corner - everyone was stunned. We chatted and I did everything you taught me when building rupport. Soon it was back to my place. She came with a date and left with me...I am the talk of my work now ha ha as I was everyone's entertainment for the night as every chode watched me in awe whilst they where there drinking beer. My Nickname is now Ken 'cos she looked just like Barbie - If the best thing they can tease me about is getting home hot girls then whatever..."

-C., Australia

"The field work was all about getting the basics right.First set(group of girls):Two set(two girls) Ozzie goes in and asks if they are Spanish (there clearly not) goes straight into rapport very high energy, very positive I enter the set we then work the girls we in the set over an hour.

Ozzie opens a mix set(a guy and a girl), I have never seem anything like it within minutes all the girls in the set are attracted to him the guys are sucking his dick . One of the girls grabs Ozzies phone and enters her number in it, her boyfriend is right in front of them!!! Ozzie is running the set high energy, positive answering questions he likes ignore the rest, Ozzie does not appear to be running any material just stories about his life.Next is my turn, Ozzie sends me into mix group(guys and girls) about six people, talk for a bit (5 -10 minutes) I'm not doing to well, they ask me who I'm with Ozzie comes in blows the set open a super hot girl (probably the hottest girl in the room at the time) who is the group comes to chat with me we talk for a while then I say something stupid (great time for a miss calibration) and talks with some else from the group.I chickening out of set so Ozzie opens another mix group three guys and girl.Its turns out the two guys are friends of the DJ and the girl is his girlfriend, after five minutes he got the guys invite to see them DJ then girl all over him and the DJ stopping playing to shake his hand......

Was the Bootcamp worth it? One word: Yes."

-G., London

"I took my Bootcamp while broke and being 17.

I had never entered a club before, I had never talkedto a girl before, I had never kissed a girl before... Well, guesswhat? I got 3 makeouts and a date with a woman from Poland, 26years old.Lol. you should've seen her face when I told her she was with anunder aged guy(boy?). I did it just for Ozzie.ohh that face, lol.Good times...Best of times?Yes. So now if YOU ask me "Was it worth it? Should I take a Bootcamp?"... Get out of my face before I kick your teeth in."

-V.B., Iceland

"I just want to pay my gratitude for Ozzie for the weekend on January the 18th-20th 2008. The results have been fascinating. The last 2-weeks have been great: I had sex with a girl from the second night and weekend after that with another girl. A couple of days ago I met this phenomenal HB girl, who looks like a model. I met her on the field and I was paying extra-attention to my rapport, calibrating between break-in rapport and neural rapport. Telling her actual stories of my everyday life in a funny manner.... I value inner game a lot and that is still the area that needs improvement, but I am on my way to massive success! Ozzie is one of the greatest persons I have ever met in my entire life, honestly. Man, I call this the life I've never had before! :)"

-Alexander. London

"I've come out of the BC with new attitudes about myself and about game. Things are a lot simpler now and I feel the path has been laid before me. All I've got to do is follow it.Let the good times roll baby!"

-T, London

"I immediately walk up behind the two girls, lean in and open them with no hesitation. They blow open completely. They start giving me birthday hugs/kisses and we start vibing. I start realising that this girl was one of, if not one of the hottest girls I've ever cold approached sober. I didn't feel any pressure what so ever. She's 25, a tall blonde with awesome blue eyes and fit as hell. I start focusing my attention on her. I notice the guy who was talking to her previously was getting threatened. Fuck him, I jump over the lounge and park myself in between him and my target. I introduce myself to him, then turned my back and started vibing with the girl. Needless to say I wouldn't hear/see the guy for the rest of the interaction.After a while I see Ozzie and he's pointing to his watch. I know what this means. Fuck. I don't want to leave, but I have to. But I know that there'll be plenty of this shit happening to me in the future. We exchange hugs and kisses. I follow Ozzie and the other students out of there.

Thanks Ozzie, for this unforgetable experience."

-Myke, Sydney

"I spent the months after going out regularly, putting in the ground work, getting sporadic results, until one night it all just seemed to click. I was on fire and made out with 8 chicks, pulling the last one back to my place. After that, things got even better, the lays started coming in and things started to get easier, I was becoming more and more congruent and the chicks loved it.

....

Thanks Ozzie for a great Bootcamp!"

-Lex, London

"Alright Guys. As you can see I am not a big Forum guy, but in this occasion I decided to share with you what are my main thoughts and concerns after taking a Bootcamp with Ozzie, one of the most genuine, dedicated and fun person I have ever met in this game. The key I would say is in this: approach without having pickup in your mind. To give an example, the second night as soon as I entered the room I was in this kind of state and as a matter of fact I was not going anywhere. After a set blew me off I stopped for a minute and told myself "Fuck Pickup. Be friendly, stop.". Luckily in that moment Ozzie sent me into a 3 set and after 5 minutes I was in, I got the number of one girl and later that night I was making out with another one of that same group who I ended up fucking her brains out on Sunday night, but that's a different story.......Now Ozzie docet (in Latin it means as Ozzie teaches...;)):

Get Physical right away. Fuck the signals......Cheers"

-Luc. Rome. Italy

"I'm a 24 year old Asian male in a wheelchair, I haven't been able to walk by birth, and I've pretty much grown up in London my whole life....First, Ozzie gave me a talk about fear...

Then came opening sets. Ozzie opened a couple making out in the middle of the street with "Hey guys, is Leicester Square actually a square??", and to my amazement, the set blew open. I then opened countless groups with that opener and was amazed at how I could still generate long conversations with almost nothing. I'd done daygame on my own before, but I only opened women on their own. I guess I couldn't handle the thought of rejection from more than just one person. Imagining people laughing about me after I tried a pathetic opening on them was more than I could ever handle. NO MORE!! Ozzie made me open couples, groups, everyone!! It was a real eye opener of how just simple opening sets with almost nothing (I mean come on!! "Is Leicester Sqaure really a square!?" and continuing to talk for a while can make them warm up to you."

-Amman, London

"Ozzie - brilliant, you can really see how he has been doing this for a while, it is so professional and I feel he knows himself and his game as well as he does the bootcamp stucture and what goes on...Ozzie says the Bootcamps are always evolving, so the next one will probably be different to the one I was on... This has singlehandedly helped my game 100 times, but the good thing is, it has also helped my confidence, how I feel and act in the world and my life! Loved it!"

-Virgo, London

"The whole weekend was a lot different to how I'd expected. All this talk of 'nimbus' and so on...didn't really get that. Ozzie was not trying to pump our state all weekend. It was actually very chilled. Instead, I just got a massive enlightenment, and learnt a lot. Ozzie is the man. The real deal."

-T.P, London

"This is bootcamp.

I've probably had 20 lays total in my life maybe more or less. Always had a problem picking up the Chicks that I wanted to have but always managed to do okay with 7s, 8s and 9s since I was 20 (Im 26 now). But I wanted more and not just women. I wanted to kill off my weaker self and be in a position to live the kind of life that I wanted to live free of internal restrictions, low-self esteem, self-doubting, fear and any form of poor mental health - however minor - that stops me from acting like a man.I found the next level through this bootcamp and I haven't even scratched the surface with this post.Nobody can be told what the matrix is Neo - they have to see it for themselves."

-S. London

"I walked over, thinking to myself 'well, that fucker can tell my mum and dad it was he who got me killed'. I walk up and shake hands with one of the guys and say 'how's it going?' Needless to say the guy was super friendly with me and we ended up talking for 10 minutes. Ozzie in the meantime came up and took the smoking hot girl off of the guy I would have sworn she was with, just to show it could be done. Again, it is realisations like this that make the bootcamp worth every penny. I would have sworn that those guys would hit me - but I'm slowly starting to realise exactly how much you can get away with in a club without any adverse effects."

-J.F., London

"In just 3 days, Ozzie has taught me so much, and helped me learn a lot about myself. When I came to the bootcamp I was expecting something big, but nothing like this, no amount of time spent reading or watching theory on this stuff can teach you what I learnt on my bootcamp!

We started chatting and dancing, and at one point Ozzie stepped behind her and was telling me to kiss her! We made out a bit, and then it was time to go, I couldve stayed with her, and taken her home, but Ozzie told me before hand, I have a choice, I could stay with any girl I picked up, or I could go debrief with him. I got her number and Ozzie and I left, I felt it was better to debrief with Ozzie while the night was still fresh, plus I was not really bothered whether I picked up a girl or not, this bootcamp was not about sex for me, but more about self actualization, and getting the freedom to talk to strangers without anxiety, and teaching myself this is possible, I can do this...I still haven't called the girl, or sent her my number, I dont know why, its like I dont really care to?"

-Goran. London.

"I wanted, and have been asked, to write up what's been happening in my life since I took Ozzie's RSD bootcamp 6 months ago. From a personal perspective, I want to be honest about it all.Anyway, this is a forum about girls so I suppose you want to know what I've been up to. Some highlights:-taking a millionairess home, via her coke dealer, disregarding the fact that she has a boyfriend. I've never seen a house so big, with so many gardens!-# closing 2 L'Oreal girls standing next to each other-# closing a girl with my left hand while I'm fingering another girl with my right-girls telling their friends to 'go home with that guy'-returning my glass of wine at the bar and swapping it for a water cos I realised I have more fun sober (so proud of that one)-pulling a 30 year old blonde to the toilets of a gay bar in Liverpool, then to the alleyway on the way home :D-having 4 dates in one week...I never had ONE date in 22 years before-getting a blowjob off a girl in Oxford who thought I was a rockstar-realizing most of the internet is full of shit-having a first date with a girl, and in 10 minutes we're having sex-having girls turn up at your house in lingerie which they've just bought for you-a girl crying cos she couldn't believe I approached her, that I am 'too hot' for her (total headfuck)-getting stopped by people who think I'm a rockstar or celebrity; getting free drinks and club entry. Girls paying for taxis so you can come to their parties...-having a girl ditch her boyfriend in the club so she can molest me instead :D

Last night, 6 months on, I have girls kicking me, grabbing me, and another girl telling me with her hand down my trousers that I'm 'the kind of guy that girls just want to grab and fuck'....Bring it on! The next 6 months are going to be awesome! I'm shooting for the very top on this one!"

-10pin, London

"Hey guys - just updating everyone here on how effective a bootcamp can be for even those people who have been in this game for a while. Been going out 2 days / week since bootcamp (7 weeks ago)

14 nights out, 6 same night lays (4 LR's on the forum, the rest still being written) 7 weeks prior to bootcamp? 1 lay Consistency? I think I'm getting there. Does the bootcamp work? See above. If you've been in this for a while, you can still learn a lot from this mind-bending experience. Thank you, Ozzie and everyone at RSD for developing such a tight program.

-The A., USA.

"Sets(groups of girls) blew open HARD. One three set I open goes so well that two of the girls eye code each other with smiles, get up and leave me with the third. They were HELPING me pick up their friend. We make out and for the rest of the night she follows me around the club yelling my name, ready to be pulled....

Another 28 year old blonde teacher that I open and vibe with, talking about shit that I enjoy in my life, goes sexual on me when I ask her what we could do for the next three minutes. Her: "We could fuck?"(INTERNALLY: WHAT THE FUCK JUST HAPPENED?!)

I feel that Oz was heavily customizing my experience. He immediately recognized what I was doing and explained how ridiculous it really was. The concept of expression, not impression had a huge impact on me and Ozzie let me know that this bootcamp was not going to be a magic pill. I will have to go through a period of delayed gratification for a while, getting no tangible success whilst I solidify my identity. I'm cool with that.On the other hand, the other students were relatively new so he was just getting them desensitized to approaching and heavy kino(Getting Physical). It was actually amazing to see some of them go from stifled and apprehensive to approaching sets like a hurricane, creating their own fun. I guess that's where the instructors get their satisfaction, seeing that kind of transformation."

-K., Sydney. Australia.

"After a demo by Ozzie we started to approach.I talked to a group of English guys that bought me an energy drink. Afterwards I talked to a sweet girl, who was in the club with her husband. She and I had a really good connection and I actually got her number with her husband standing right next to us. And he was just super friendly to me despite of this.

We then went extreme with the physical as he wanted me to try to break up a guy and a girl making out. He showed me how to do it first, by breaking up a guy and a girl that were kissing. He talked to the guy first and then clawed the girl HARD. She got away from Ozzie, but he still tried to pull her back while she pinched his nipples..."

-G. London

"I was 18 and had just moved to Russia for studies. I was overwhelmed by the vast number of hot women there... they were everywhere, literally everywhere...

The true value of the bootcamp was in the field time, I cant even put it in words how effective it is for your progress, to have an instructor teaching you the right things every second... This shit would have taken a lot of time and patience to learn by myself. I am really grateful that I got it so simplified, and especially at such a young age... Ozzie is one hell of an instructor and is very dedicated... he takes coaching very seriously. His bootcamp has probabaly changed and evolved now but it can only have been for the better, so I highly recommend it to anyone and everyone."

-**Bartel B. St. Petersburg. Russia.**